M000202587

THE
[E S S E N T I A L]
[QUESTION]

HOW YOU CAN MAKE A DIFFERENCE FOR GOD

WHITNEY T. KUNIHOLM

A 10-WEEK BIBLE READING EXPERIENCE

IVP Books

An imprint of InterVarsity Press
Downers Grove, Illinois

InterVarsity Press
P.O. Box 1400, Downers Grove, IL 60515-1426
World Wide Web: www.ivpress.com
Email: email@ivpress.com

©2014 by Whitney T. Kuniholm

All rights reserved. No part of this book may be reproduced in any form without written permission from InterVarsity Press.

InterVarsity Press® is the book-publishing division of InterVarsity Christian Fellowship/USA®, a movement of students and faculty active on campus at hundreds of universities, colleges and schools of nursing in the United States of America, and a member movement of the International Fellowship of Evangelical Students. For information about local and regional activities, write Public Relations Dept., InterVarsity Christian Fellowship/USA, 6400 Schroeder Rd., P.O. Box 7895, Madison, WI 53707-7895, or visit the IVCF website at www.intervarsity.org.

All Scripture quotations, unless otherwise indicated, are taken from the Holy Bible, New International Version®. NIV®. *Copyright ©1973, 1978, 1984 by International Bible Society. Used by permission of Zondervan Publishing House. All rights reserved.*

While all stories in this book are true, some names and identifying information in this book have been changed to protect the privacy of the individuals involved.

Cover design: Crosssection
Interior design: Beth Hagenberg
Images: Hikage Keita

ISBN 978-0-8308-3674-1 (print)
ISBN 978-0-8308-9666-0 (digital)

Printed in the United States of America ∞

 As a member of the Green Press Initiative, InterVarsity Press is committed to protecting the environment and to the responsible use of natural resources. To learn more, visit greenpressinitiative.org.

Library of Congress Cataloging-in-Publication Data

Kuniholm, Whitney T.
  The essential question : how you can make a difference for God / Whitney T. Kuniholm.
    pages cm
  Includes bibliographical references.
  ISBN 978-0-8308-3674-1 (pbk. : alk. paper)
  1. *Bible. Acts--Devotional literature. I. Title.*
BS2625.54.K86 2014
226.6'06--dc23

                                                                    2014012653

P 21 20 19 18 17 16 15 14 13 12 11 10 9 8 7 6 5 4 3 2 1

Y 31 30 29 28 27 26 25 24 23 22 21 20 19 18 17 16 15 14

For my friends and colleagues in Scripture Union,

a ministry team that's making a difference for

God around the world every day

CONTENTS

INTRODUCTION

I don't want to look back someday and realize I wasted my time. I want my life to count for something important.

This world is a very needy place. If my Christian faith means anything at all, I've got to figure out what I can do about it.

Honestly, what motivates me is not guilt. I want to help others because I'm so thankful for what God has done for me.

People think that having a "mission from God" is a joke. Not me. It's what I've always wanted.

There are so many ways to make a difference in the world. How do I know what God wants me to do?

What difference am I making with my life? Have you ever asked yourself that? Of course you have! On some level, every human being is struggling to find their own answer to that fundamental question. In fact, I believe the search for significance is the underlying motivation for virtually all human activity. It's what drives us.

Most people want to make a *positive* impact with their lives—through education, career, family, service to the community or through accomplishing some notable goal or achievement. Even those who are headed in a *negative* direction, like criminals or gang members, are still attempting to make an impact with their lives; they want to be recognized and they want to be respected.

While it's true that we get distracted on our search by any number of contemporary temptations, nonetheless, human beings seem to have a built-in longing to make their lives count for something more. The philosopher Plato reportedly described the human as "a being in search of meaning." And in more recent times, Viktor Frankl, a survivor of the Nazi concentration camps and author of the classic book *Man's Search for Meaning*, wrote, "Man's main concern is not to gain pleasure or to avoid pain but rather to see a meaning in his life."[1]

But for Christians, there's an extra dimension. If you are a follower of Jesus, you know that life is more than what you have or what you accomplish or even what people think of you. For Christians, the real question is: How can I make a difference *for God?* Jesus gave us the answer in his Sermon on the Mount: "Seek first his kingdom and his righteousness" (Matthew 6:33). That's our mission statement. Regardless of what happens in this life, all believers are headed to the same finish line, where we're hoping to hear our Heavenly Father say, "Well done, good and faithful servant!" (Matthew 25:21). Isn't that what you're really longing for?

A JOURNEY TOGETHER

"Yes, I do want to make a difference for God," you may be thinking, "but *how can I?*" That's a very important question, and it's the one I want to help you answer in this book. To do that I want to take a journey with you through the New Testament book of Acts, one of the most exciting reads in the entire Bible.

Let me say right up front, I'm not a theologian or a scholar. So if you're looking for a heavy doctrinal treatise on the subject, you won't find it here. I'm simply a follower of Jesus who believes that God's Word still speaks today, if we are willing to listen. And I believe the book of Acts is the perfect place to start our journey, because it tells the story of how the first Christians, both individuals and small groups, struggled to answer the question, how can we make a difference for God?

THE ESSENTIAL QUESTION

In Acts 22 there is a very significant passage that will become the theme of our journey together. The apostle Paul was in Jerusalem when the religious leaders stirred up a riot against him because he had been preaching the good news about Jesus Christ. Before things got completely out of hand, a Roman commander arrested Paul, effectively rescuing him from the violent mob (see Acts 21:27-40). But instead of playing it safe, Paul asked to speak to the angry crowd, and when he was given permission he recounted his own conversion experience (Acts 22:3-21).

Paul explained that several years earlier he had been traveling to the town of Damascus when he was overwhelmed by a blinding light and heard a voice from heaven. In response he asked two questions. The first was, "Who are you, Lord?" (Acts 22:8). Paul didn't immediately realize it, but he was having an encounter with Jesus.

The second question—and the one we'll wrestle with in this book—was, "What shall I do, Lord?" (Acts 22:10). Lying in the dust on the Damascus road, Paul articulated the question every believer must answer; it is the *essential question*. Once we've encountered Jesus and made our decision to follow him, the next question must be, "What shall I do, Lord?"

It's fascinating to read how God answered. "'Get up,' the Lord said, 'and go into Damascus. There you will be told all that you have been assigned to do'" (Acts 22:10). Think about that for a minute. God had an *assignment* for Paul. Could it be that he also has an assignment for all Christians, including you and me? I believe the answer is yes. As we'll discover in the experiences of the first Christians, God has a mission, an essential mission, for his people.

That doesn't mean your mission will be as remarkable as Paul's. In fact, it probably won't be. Yes, God may call you to serve him in short-term missions, or even in a full-time missionary career. And if he does, that would be wonderful! But it's just as likely, and just as important, that God will call you to serve him faithfully in the marketplace, in the home, in school, in the military or someplace else. We must never forget that meeting the practical and spiritual needs of the people around us is an enormously valuable and often over-looked mission. And we can do that no matter what "day job" we may have. As the prophet Micah said, "And what does the LORD require of you? To act justly and to love mercy and to walk humbly with your God" (Micah 6:8).

So our challenge as we work our way through the book of Acts is not to feel pressured to outdo the apostle Paul's missionary accomplishments. Rather, it's to answer the essential question for ourselves—that is, to find and follow God's assignment for us today.

ABOUT THE HOLY SPIRIT

Before we begin our journey, there's something else I want to clarify. When people consider the book of Acts, they often think of one thing: that Day of Pentecost when God poured out his Holy Spirit. To be sure, the work of the Holy Spirit is a major theme in Acts. But there's more to the book than just chapter 2—much more, as you will see.

Today the Holy Spirit has become a much-debated issue in the church. Some Christians seem to emphasize him too much and slip into excess. Others seem to keep him on the sidelines, as if he no longer exists. And both sides seem suspicious of the other. So let me put you at ease: I don't have an agenda on either side. I'm hoping we can avoid that controversy, mostly because it will distract us from our essential question.

With that in mind, I want to ask you to affirm two things with me. First, let's agree that the Holy Spirit is one person of our triune God. As it says in the Nicene Creed, "We believe in the Holy Spirit, the Lord, the giver of life, who proceeds from the Father and the Son. With the Father and the Son he is worshiped and glorified." And second, let's agree to let the text of Scripture form our understanding of how the Holy Spirit works. In other words, let's allow God's Word to be our teacher.

HOW TO USE THIS BOOK

At this point you may be thinking, "Of course I want to make a difference for God. But honestly, I'm not sure I'll be able to stick with this regular Bible reading thing." If that's how you feel, don't worry; most people struggle with Bible reading. That's why I've designed this book to make your journey through Acts easy and meaningful. Let me make a few suggestions that will get you off to a good start.

First, *The Essential Question* is designed to be used with a Bible. Each chapter tells you what passage to read and then helps you think about the main points. Obviously, if you don't read each Bible passage *The Essential Question* won't make much sense. But one good thing is that you can use any Bible translation you want. I recommend, however, that you use one of the many excellent modern translations, such as the *New International Version* (NIV), the *New Revised Standard Version* (NRSV), the *English Standard Version* (ESV), the *Holman Christian Standard Bible* (HCSB), the *New American Bible, Revised Edition* (NABRE) or the *New Living Translation* (NLT). If you are still unsure about which Bible translation to use, you might want to check with a pastor, minister or priest.

Second, *The Essential Question* guides you through fifty short passages in the book of Acts. The readings are undated so you can complete them at any pace—fifty days, ten weeks, a year or more. But whatever schedule you pick, don't feel guilty if you miss a day. Just do the next reading whenever you have time and before you know it you'll make it through all fifty. Also, I've grouped the readings into sets of five and included introductions that point out important themes. This might help you do one set of five readings each week.

Third, you will notice that for each reading I've followed a four-step process. I begin with an opening statement, prayer thought or question intended to help you *prepare* for the study. Next I list the Bible passage, which you should *read*, perhaps a few times, before proceeding. The most important part of this entire journey is that you read God's Word for yourself. After that, I offer you my own comments on the text to help you *reflect* on the passage, especially keeping in mind our desire to make a difference for God. But don't let me do all the work! You need to ask yourself: What do I think is the main point of this passage? And what is God saying to me about the work he has called me to do? Finally, for each reading I offer an idea on how to *apply* the passage. I've tried to make these action oriented, because I've learned the best way to really understand the Bible is to live it out.

At the back of this book you'll find a useful feature, the Essential Question Journal. As you take this journey, use this space often to jot down your insights from the Bible or your responses to the essential question. At the end of the study, you'll have a record of what God has been saying to you.

One more thing: I would strongly recommend that you wrap this Bible reading process in prayer. Before you start each passage, ask God to help you understand his Word. You may want to spend a few minutes in thanksgiving, confession or praise. Remember, you're beginning a dialogue, not just a discipline. Then after you complete your reading and reflection, pray again, this time asking God to help you obey his Word. Turn the things you've learned into prayers. Also pray about your own needs and the needs of others. And be sure to thank God for any answers to prayer you've experienced recently.

DON'T GO IT ALONE

At the end of each section I've included a page of discussion questions. Why? Because *the best way to take this journey is with another person, or better yet, with a small group.* Each week, try to complete a set of five readings on your own. Then get together with your friend or group to talk about what you've learned. Start by encouraging each person to share their own insights from the readings. Use the discussion questions to continue the conversation. You'll find that reading and discussing the Bible with others creates positive motivation to keep going and makes your experience of God's Word more meaningful.

Another excellent way to use this book is to have your entire church congregation read *The Essential Question* together. Ask your pastor, minister or priest to get behind this program and work with others in the church to encourage everyone to participate. Over the years I've seen that a tremendous spiritual energy is unleashed when a congregation commits themselves to reading and living God's Word together; I call it "Bible reading revival." Imagine if your church went through *The Essential Question* and then worked together to make a difference for God in your community. (To learn more about the range of resources available from Scripture Union to make *The Essential Question* a successful church-wide Bible reading experience, see page 143.)

THE MOST IMPORTANT THING

As you're about to discover, the book of Acts tells the story of how the first Christians attempted to answer the essential question, that is, to find out what God wanted them to do in their world. But having a better understanding of how *they did it* is only part of what we want to accomplish on our journey. The most important thing is to discover how *you'll do it*, how you'll begin to make a difference for God today. Ultimately, that's why you picked up this book: because you want to make your life count for God now.

So my prayer is that over the next ten weeks, or however long it takes for you to complete this journey, you'll get a better understanding of the assignment—whether great or small—God has for you. And more than that, I pray you'll have the faith and courage to wholeheartedly pursue it, because that's how, with God's help, you could change your world forever.

Part One

THE ESSENTIAL COMMUNITY

[WEEK ONE]

The Church Is Born

The book of Acts tells the second-most exciting story in the Bible. The most exciting story, of course, is God becoming a human being by entering the world he created in the person of Jesus Christ. But Acts is the great sequel to the gospel. It addresses the question, what happened after Jesus left earth? What happened is that the church was born and against all odds began its unstoppable, global growth and development. That's the story we're about to begin.

You're probably already familiar with the dramatic highlights in Acts, and there are many—the ascension, the Day of Pentecost, Peter's early leadership and miraculous experiences, Paul's conversion and missionary journeys. But there are also many less dramatic passages in Acts, and there's a lot to be learned from them too. How did the early church function day-to-day? How did the first Christians make decisions together? How did they resolve conflicts? By examining both the familiar and the overlooked passages in Acts, we'll discover some principles that can help us make a difference for God today.

In these first five passages, we'll read about the first decision the early Christians made after Jesus returned to heaven: who would replace Judas? The way they went about it gives us a model for discerning God's will today. Next we'll read about the Day of Pentecost, the time when God poured out his Holy Spirit and gave birth to the church. That was a lot for the small group of Christians to absorb, so God inspired Peter to explain what was going on in one of the greatest impromptu sermons ever. Discerning God's will, relying on the Holy Spirit, perceiving how God is at work—these are all critical spiritual abilities for those who want to make a difference for God today.

But the most amazing thing about the book of Acts is that the story isn't over. The church is still growing and developing—and you're part of that story. So let's get going!

DAY ONE: The Essential Truth

Prepare: How have you made a difference for God with your life so far?

Read: Acts 1:1-11

Reflect: Luke is on his second career. He started out as a physician; now he's a writer (1:1). Why? Because he encountered Jesus. His new passion is telling the story of the man who changed his life. Compared to that, everything else is secondary. But that's what it means to be a Christian: you have a new passion in life—Jesus. He becomes your first priority.

The book of Acts is the sequel to Luke's Gospel, and Luke begins in the typical way, with a look back to where his first book left off— with the death and resurrection of Jesus (Acts 1:3-5; see Luke 22–24). It would be easy to breeze past this review, but we'd miss an important point: the first step to making a difference for God is being sure of the "many convincing proofs that he [Jesus] was alive" (1:3). Are you sure of this?

As we begin this journey through Acts, ask yourself, what's my real motivation for wanting to serve God? Is it gratitude for all he's done? Concern for a world in need? A desire to respond to his call? That's all good. But if, like the disciples, it's a desire to push some other agenda, whether personal or political, that's not so good. So take time to prayerfully ask, are my priorities fully aligned with God's? Being a little off track now could take you way off course down the road.

What I find most intriguing about this passage is the insight it gives us into the disciples' mindset. When they had a chance to talk in private with the resurrected Jesus, their first concern was national issues (1:6). Jesus wanted to give them spiritual power so they could change the world (8), but all they wanted was political power so they could be in charge (6). Go figure. That's why Jesus made clear that the Holy Spirit was not coming to make them more prominent. Instead, he would make them more effective by empowering their witness (8). That's still the key to making a difference for God.

Luke ends his introduction by setting the stage for an even more dramatic sequel. Someday Jesus will come back, and when he does, it's going to be big, really big (11). This passage reminds us that the essential truth of the Christian faith is this: Christ has died. Christ is risen. Christ will come again.

Apply: Take some time today to jot down the "chapter headings" or stages in your life story. Is there a chapter on how you encountered Jesus? If so, what difference has it made?

DAY TWO: So, Now What?

Prepare: Spend some time praising God, either in silent prayer or aloud, or perhaps by humming or singing a favorite praise song with your eyes closed.

Read: Acts 1:12-26

Reflect: When I was in elementary school I went to Camp Passumpsic, a boys' camp in rural Vermont. For two summers I loved it because we did lots of fun things—hiking, archery, sailing and swimming in Lake Fairlee. But during my third summer at Passumpsic something unexpected happened. Our cabin counselor quit, right in the middle of the season! When Uncle Cal, the camp director, shared the news, we were shocked. So, now what?

Maybe that's a little like what these first Christians felt in Acts 1. For three years they had been on an exciting ride with Jesus, listening to his teaching, witnessing his miracles, agonizing over his death, rejoicing at his resurrection. Then he disappeared. They had to be thinking, *so, now what?*

What do you do when you don't know what to do? For example, when you lose your job, when a relationship ends, when your life takes an unexpected turn? The early believers didn't have all the answers as they returned to Jerusalem, but they instinctively knew the best response to uncertainty: they got together for prayer and praise (Acts 1:14; Luke 24:52-53). Often God gives clarity to our minds as we worship him from our hearts.

At first glance, "casting lots" may seem like a strange way to choose a replacement for Judas (1:26). But the practice was used in the Old Testament as a way of receiving direction from God (Leviticus 16:8; Numbers 26:55; Proverbs 16:33), so for these believers it wouldn't have seemed odd. However, after the coming of the Spirit, casting lots seems not to have been used in this way.

A careful look at this passage shows that this little band of believers also searched for God's direction in a variety of other ways. Notice that they were guided by Scripture (1:20), used common sense (1:21-22) and spent time in prayer (1:24-25). When all three of these elements point in the same direction, we can trust that God is leading us.

In the middle of the passage Luke includes a fascinating detail that reveals a lot about how God works: the believers numbered "about a hundred and twenty" (1:15). You would think God's strategy for changing the world would include talented leaders, great programs and lots of resources. Sometimes it does. But here, God was planning to use a small, unknown group, about the size of an average church today, to bring his good news "to the ends of the earth" (1:8). The only way they could ever hope to pull it off was to rely on God's power, not their own, as we'll soon find out.

Apply: What is the area of greatest uncertainty in your life right now? Write it down on a 3" x 5" card. Then over the next week, on the back of the card add insights from Scripture, common sense and prayer that relate to the topic. At the end of the week, share with a trusted Christian friend what God has been saying to you.

DAY THREE: The Real, Real World

Prepare: What do you believe about the Holy Spirit? How have you experienced the Holy Spirit?

Read: Acts 2:1-13

Reflect: Imagine sitting in your church at Christmas or Easter when all of a sudden you hear a loud noise that's not coming from the sound system. Small flames mysteriously appear in midair and move around the sanctuary on their own. Then, people who quietly sit in their same pew every week stand up and start preaching in another language. You'd nervously look at the clergy and realize, *Uh oh. They didn't plan this.*

Most people today believe God exists. Christians go further and put him at the center of their lives and worldview. But when we have direct experiences of God at work, it can be unsettling, like watching a lion escape from the zoo. Notice how this initial group of believers and seekers reacted to "the wonders of God" (2:11): they were bewildered, amazed and perplexed (2:6, 7, 12). Our first reaction to the work of the Holy Spirit, then and now, shouldn't be to theologize. Rather, it should be to worship. God is here now; that's still the main thing we need to know.

But I wonder if the way we typically understand this Day of Pentecost is a little backward. Of course it's natural for us to think God intervened in *our world* by pouring out his Spirit, and there's a sense in which that's true. But maybe a better perspective is to see this event as a glimpse into *God's world*, the world where God the Father, God the Son and God the Holy Spirit are eternally present. That's the *real*, real world, which Jesus has opened to his followers forever.

Next, let's not miss the significance of a mundane phrase at the beginning of this dramatic account: "They were all together in one place" (2:1). Even though they didn't have their own building, they did have something more important: a commitment to being together. And how many were present? At least the twelve, and probably the 120 mentioned earlier (1:15), plus a crowd of God-fearing Jews (2:5). But the point is, it wasn't a megachurch. Further, they didn't pretend to understand everything that was happening. At this point their theology was simply, "What does this mean?" (2:12). And yet God used them to launch the next great move in his plan of salvation, the birth of the church.

Passionate followers of Jesus, waiting on the Lord, empowered by the Holy Spirit, even when they don't have all the answers—that's God's formula for changing the world.

Apply: If you have time, do a study of the word *Spirit*, using a concordance or an online Bible. If you don't have time, review the following passages: Genesis 1:2; Psalm 139:7-10; Joel 2:28-32; John 14:15-31; Galatians 5:16-26.

DAY FOUR: What Just Happened?

Prepare: What is the clearest evidence of God's work in your life over the last twelve months? What are the biggest challenges you face over the next twelve months?

Read: Acts 2:14-36

Reflect: After the initial fireworks on the Day of Pentecost, there must have been a stunned silence. *What just happened?* It's often difficult to understand what God is doing in the "real time" of our lives. Usually we see the pattern as we look back from the perspective of a few more years. That's why it's good to take time to remember, perhaps by writing in a notebook or journal, God's work in the past. It helps us to become more assured that he will work in the future, no matter how dark the clouds may seem.

In the crucial moments after the Spirit was poured out, those present needed to understand what God was doing and how it connected to God's past work. Peter wasted no time in providing the necessary leadership: he stood up and addressed the crowd (2:14). Maybe this reflected his natural tendency to be the first to take action in any situation. That can be a strength, and a weakness (see John 18:10). More likely Peter's response showed that this rough and ready fisherman had spent three years with a certain Scripture-focused carpenter from Nazareth (Acts 4:13). Getting to know Jesus and gaining an understanding of God's Word is still critical to becoming an effective spiritual leader.

Peter proceeded to preach one of the most powerful sermons in the history of the church, and that without the help of a microphone, PowerPoint or teleprompter. First, he interpreted the events the crowd had just witnessed: they are the fulfillment of a message from the Old Testament prophet Joel (Acts 2:17-21; see Joel 2:28-31). Next, Peter summarized the ministry of Jesus and explained its connection to the Holy Spirit (2:22-33). And finally, he concluded that "God has made this Jesus ... Lord and Christ" (2:36). In other words, Jesus was the Anointed One, the Messiah, the culmination of God's plan to save the world from sin. Peter understood that the Holy Spirit was proof that it was all true.

But what do we make of the seemingly offensive zinger Peter added to his closing statement: "whom you crucified" (2:36)? The fact is, Peter lived in the same community with those who killed Jesus; he knew these guys (2:14). Maybe his comment wasn't an accusation as much as an explanation: *Look, I know what you were thinking when you went after Jesus, but here's what really went down.*

Making a difference for God starts when we are willing to speak about Jesus to the people closest to us, our family and people in our neighborhood. That can be difficult and must always be done in love. But when we develop the courage and clarity to show the ones closest to us that we're all in with Jesus, it becomes easier to share the good news with others who are farther away.

Apply: Think back to opportunities you've had to explain the gospel to others. What seemed most effective for you? Now pray for one opportunity this week to have an effective faith-based conversation.

DAY FIVE: The New Testament Church

Prepare: Spend a few moments thanking God for your church, its leaders, ministry and congregation. Ask God to increase its impact in the area where you live.

Read: Acts 2:37-47

Reflect: I went to a Christian college in the mid-1970s, and sometimes the "radical" students on campus would vent their frustration with the college church. "Why do we have to go there?" they'd say. "Why can't we just get back to being *a New Testament church*?" It all sounded very spiritual, but over time I realized that for some the real concern wasn't to recover the original vision of the church, it was to sleep in on Sunday mornings. So what was the New Testament church really like?

In some ways the answer is easy. Luke mentions four defining activities: teaching, fellowship, eating and prayer (2:42). But hold on—aren't all of those present in most churches today (especially the third one)? So why does the church in the West continue to experience decline? Maybe the answer is that we have all the right activities but we've lost touch with the deeper realities that made these first Christians successful. Let's take a look at four of these realities from this passage.

Priority. There was no question that Jesus was the church's main focus (2:36-39). They had seen and heard him "live" for three years; many were eyewitnesses of his resurrection. What could be more important than continuing to follow him? The starting point for any group of Christians that wants to make a difference today is laser-like alignment with Jesus.

Power. The spectacular growth of the church (2:41, 47) wasn't a human phenomenon. God was at work in very clear and powerful ways (2:43). We must be careful not to package or sensationalize the work of the Holy Spirit today. But we should also not assume he isn't still active. The best attitude is one of humble openness to whatever God chooses to do in his church.

Community. Luke highlights the togetherness of these believers, a theme he mentions three times in six verses (2:42-47). Today there are many sophisticated strategies for helping churches grow, but certainly one of the simplest is for congregations to do more things together. Perhaps worship, fellowship and prayer that involve all age groups are more important to the spiritual health of churches and families than we realize.

Responsiveness. When the people heard the good news preached, they gave a response that evangelists today dream about: they asked, "What shall we do?" (2:37). A healthy church is one where people know they need forgiveness and are quick to repent (2:38). That opens the way for even greater blessing and effectiveness.

So today when we say, "Let's just get back to the New Testament church," we need to remember it will require a combination of the right activities and the right underlying motivations. But that's what will cause the church to grow and make a difference in the world.

Apply: Sometime today, send a note or an email of encouragement to the pastor(s) at your church and let them know you are praying for them.

DISCUSSION QUESTIONS

After you've completed the five readings in the section "The Church Is Born," get together with another person or group to talk about what you've learned. Begin by sharing the insights you've gained from your own reflection on the passages. Then use the following questions to help you continue the conversation.

1. In what ways have you encountered Jesus in your life? Would you consider yourself a follower of Jesus today? Explain. (Acts 1:1-11)

2. What are you most passionate about in life? What are your top priorities for the next few years? How does your relationship with Jesus affect your priorities? (Acts 1:1-11)

3. What are the biggest decisions you've had to make in your life? How did you make them? What were the results? (Acts 1:12-26)

4. What principles do you use for determining God's will for your life now? (Acts 1:12-26)

5. What have you learned and what have you experienced of the Holy Spirit? How could you be more open to his work in your life? (Acts 2:1-13)

6. For you, what does it mean to wait on the Lord? When and how have you done this, and what was the result? What happens when you *don't* wait on the Lord? (Acts 2:1-13)

7. Who do you influence with your life? Who is affected by your example? How could you become a better spiritual leader within your circle of influence? (Acts 2:14-36)

8. Have you ever had the opportunity to share what you believe

about Jesus with your family or close friends? How did you feel, and how did it go? What have you learned about effectively sharing the good news with others? (Acts 2:14-36)

9. Do you think it's important for churches and families to spend more time in all-age worship, fellowship and prayer? Why? (Acts 2:37-47)

10. What are some ideas for doing more things together with people in your church? Or in your family? (Acts 2:37-47)

[Week Two]

The Church Begins to Grow

Have you ever been part of something that was really successful? Maybe you were on a team that won the championship. Maybe your business experienced a time of incredible sales and profitability. Or perhaps you put something on the Internet that went viral. Whatever it was, it's exciting when something you are part of begins to grow.

Our next five readings take us to an exhilarating growth phase in the life of the early church. The first Christians were still riding the wave of the Holy Spirit that was poured out on the Day of Pentecost. As a result, their witness for Christ was clear and effective. Not only that, God was healing people and performing miraculous signs and wonders through the name of Jesus (Acts 4:30). The church was on a roll.

One thing you'll want pay attention to in Acts 3–4 is the clues these chapters give us about how the early church operated. We notice that their main focus was Jesus, and their main activities were prayer, worship and caring for one another. Because of this, the Holy Spirit did some incredible things. We may not be able to exactly replicate the New Testament church today, but we can identify the principles that were at work then and apply them now.

Another theme to watch for is the way the early Christians instinctively blended spiritual and practical concerns. For them, there was no divide between evangelism and social action, between witnessing for Christ and helping the needy. Getting that balance right has been a challenge for the church through the ages. But as you'll see, the early Christians didn't seem to struggle with it. Blending the two concerns came naturally for them.

Finally, several of our readings feature the dynamic duo of Peter and John. They had emerged as leaders in the early church, which gave them some high-profile opportunities to speak and heal. But they also began to attract the attention of the religious establishment. At this time there was no significant opposition. That would come soon enough. But one lesson we'll take away from these readings is that whenever we're part of something God is blessing, we can expect spiritual opposition. It goes with the territory.

There's a sense in which these next five readings cover the high point for the church in the book of Acts. God is blessing them, their numbers are growing and they aren't experiencing much opposition. But a good question to ask is, what is success? Is it growth in numbers and giving? Is it high visibility in the community? Is it the absence of opposition? As you continue thinking about how you can make a difference for God today, see if you figure out God's definition of a successful ministry.

DAY SIX: "Just Do It" Faith

Prepare: Spend some time thanking God for healings you're aware of and asking him for healings that are still needed.

Read: Acts 3:1-10

Reflect: I could have told Peter and John they were making a big mistake. *Don't make eye contact with panhandlers. If you do, you'll go broke!* But it's obvious that the apostles weren't worried about money;

they didn't have any! What they cared about was making a difference in the life of this crippled man so that more people would learn about Jesus Christ (3:6). If you want to have an impact in the lives of those around you, maybe you'll need to become less concerned about the things of this world and more concerned about the things of God.

This passage also marks another small turning point in the book of Acts. Up until now, the first Christians had functioned like a private home group. But here the church began to enter the public square. Whether Peter and John realized it, God's vision of the church was not that it remained a little club of people who gathered to reminisce about the good old days with Jesus. Instead, it was going to become a global movement of people who were willing to let God use them to share the good news about Jesus with others.

Now think about the main point of this passage: the crippled man was healed, a fact that got everyone's attention (3:9-10). If it were me, I'd have had lots of questions. *Are you sure we should be doing this? What if nothing happens? What will people think?* But the text gives no hint that Peter had any second thoughts. Instead, it says, "Peter looked straight at him" (3:4) and grabbed him "by the right hand" (3:7). Those are the observations of an eyewitness. Sometimes it's better not to over-think our efforts to serve others. We'll probably get more done for God if we have a little more of Peter's "just do it" faith.

I love the reaction of the healed man, jumping for joy in the temple courts (3:8). Have you ever felt that sense of unrestrained delight in your church? For the healed man it was a natural reaction to having his long-term physical problem solved. But it was more than that; he was also praising God. In the healing he had experienced the God of the universe for himself. For the rest of his life, every step he took would remind him of that encounter.

Peter and John hadn't set out on a healing mission; they were just going to an afternoon prayer meeting. But they were willing to respond with action-oriented faith to the curbside opportunity God put in front of them. That's still a good way to make a difference for God.

Apply: Make a list of the things that remind you that God is real and active in your life, and then put it in a visible spot. Whenever you see it throughout the day take a moment to praise God.

DAY SEVEN: The Hard Sayings of Peter

Prepare: Pray for some people you know who are resistant to the good news about Jesus Christ.

Read: Acts 3:11-26

Reflect: I wonder if any church today would appoint Peter as its denominational leader. First of all, he was a fisherman, not a seminary graduate (Matthew 4:18-20). Second, Peter had recently been part of a violent altercation involving weapons (John 18:10). Finally, there were legitimate questions about his commitment to Christ (Matthew 26:69-75). *Maybe we should look at other candidates.* But Jesus saw in Peter someone he could build on (Matthew 16:18), and in this passage we begin to see why.

What's interesting is that Peter wasn't afraid of the limelight, nor was he tempted by it (Acts 3:11-12). Either of those two tendencies can undercut our ability to communicate the gospel. In addition, in the midst of dramatic ministry results Peter stayed on message. He knew that it wasn't about him; it was all about Jesus (3:16).

Even so, Peter was able to say some hard things when necessary. Modern psychologists encourage us to use "I statements" when having a difficult conversation: I was perplexed. I can't understand. I felt offended. That wasn't Peter's way. He preferred "you statements" to convict his audience: *You handed him over. You disowned him. You killed him* (3:13-15). Maybe Peter had earned the right to be so direct about the failings of others because he had confronted the same issues in his own life (John 18:15-18).

Yet the deeper motivation for Peter's tough message was not just judgment; it was a genuine concern for the eternal destiny of his listeners. He started by connecting Jesus to Jewish history, identifying him as the servant of "the God of Abraham, Isaac and Jacob" (3:13). People are more likely to listen if we take time to understand their context first. Next, Peter gave them some moral wiggle room, suggesting that they had "acted in ignorance" when they crucified Jesus (3:17). Being gracious never hurts. And finally, Peter suggested clear action steps to faith in Jesus and pointed to a positive benefit (3:19). These principles can help us more effectively share our faith today.

There's one more thing that made Peter an effective spokesman for the early church: he believed Jesus was coming back (3:21). He even addressed the doubts some had, then and now, about the second coming by pointing to Scripture. Abraham, Moses and "all the prophets" (3:18) have been telling the same story for generations: God has a plan of salvation that culminates in the birth, death and resurrection of his Son, Jesus Christ. Knowing that big story of the Bible is how you too can become an effective spokesperson for Christ.

Apply: Sometime today, read Luke 24:13-35. How does this passage affect your understanding of the big story of the Bible and your understanding of Jesus?

DAY EIGHT: The Offense of Christianity

Prepare: Spend some time thanking God for the things you know are true about him.

Read: Acts 4:1-22

Reflect: Here we go again. The religious leaders were opposing the apostles just as they had done with Jesus. But the source of their irritation, at least to begin with, was not personal; it was theological. The Sadducees didn't believe in life after death. That's why "proclaiming in

Jesus the resurrection of the dead" (4:2) was like waving a red flag at a
bull. But behind this theological concern was a darker motive, the raw
desire for power and control (4:7). As the rulers, elders and teachers
of the law piled on with the Sadducees the next day (4:5), we have a
sense of what's coming, and it doesn't look good for Peter and John.

Why is it that through the ages some people have been so irritated
by those who follow Jesus? Perhaps Peter put his finger on the answer
with his bold assertion in verse 12: there's only one way to find salvation—faith in Jesus. That truth has been called the offense of Christianity, and it still rankles modern, pluralistic minds. People are willing
to accept a bland "Christian universalism." But the exclusive claims of
the gospel make otherwise tolerant blood boil.

The question we must ask is, how do we know it's true that Jesus is
the only way to God? The answer has several parts. First, there are
Jesus' own words: "I am the way and the truth and the life. No one
comes to the Father except through me" (John 14:6). Second, the
miracles of Jesus, and as we begin to see in Acts, those of his followers
(Acts 4:14), are confirmation of the truth. Third, the resurrection of
Jesus, a fact attested to by many eyewitnesses, is a powerful validation
(1 Corinthians 15:3-8). Fourth, there is the evidence of changed lives
(Acts 4:13). Fifth, there is the death-defying courage and conviction
of Jesus' followers (4:8-12, 19-20). Ultimately, however, the most convincing proof is the unvarnished testimony of Christians through the
centuries, people who have been willing to share their experience of
Jesus with others no matter what the cost.

Even so, there's no excuse for Christians to be arrogant or inten-
tionally offensive. We must always speak the truth in love (Ephesians
4:15). When we don't, even the good news becomes nothing more than
an irritating background noise (1 Corinthians 13:1).

Apply: Think of a non-Christian friend and try to verbalize how you'd
explain to them that salvation is found in no one else besides Jesus.

DAY NINE: Fearless Prayer

Prepare: If you can, go to a window, look at the sky and pray, "Be exalted, O God, above the heavens; let your glory be over all the earth" (Psalm 108:5).

Read: Acts 4:23-31

Reflect: A few years ago I was playing golf by myself on a drizzly day at the Maumee Bay Golf Course in Ohio. On the fifteenth hole, a par three, I hit a five-wood to the front of the green, then watched as the ball rolled toward the pin and dropped into the cup. My first ever hole-in-one—but no one saw it! When I got to the clubhouse I went to the pro shop manager and told him my incredible news. "Humph," he said, barely looking up from his papers, "that's a hard hole."

Who do you call when you have exciting news to share? Your spouse, your parents, maybe a close friend? As soon as Peter and John hit the street they reported back to "their own people" (4:23), that is, the church. They weren't interested in getting attention for themselves. Rather, they were interested in sharing the good news about Jesus. That's still what makes the church effective. But the majority of this passage records how these believers prayed in response to opposition. Let's take a closer look, because it gives us insight into the mind and heart of this essential church.

Notice they started by focusing on God, not their problems (4:24). Often when I pray, I go straight to what's bothering me, and there's nothing wrong with that (see Psalm 68:19). But if I'm not careful, my prayer becomes more like obsessing on my worries than talking to God. That's why it helps me to look into the sky sometimes as I pray. I'm reminded that God is bigger than my problems.

But the most interesting thing about this prayer is what the church didn't ask God for: *safety*. You'd think that after being harassed and mistreated, they'd have been scared, especially since they knew what happened to Jesus. But there's not even a hint of fear in this prayer. In fact, what they ask for is spiritual boldness (4:29)—and this request isn't out of spiritual bravado, either. That's because their primary concern wasn't for protection or even for their rights. Rather, it was for greater effectiveness in sharing the good news. That's the secret of fearless prayer, and it's a key ingredient for those who want to make a difference for God today.

Apply: Are you facing a situation that intimidates or scares you? Ask God to help you overcome fear and boldly trust him to work through you.

DAY TEN: The Perfect Church

Prepare: Have you ever been part of a church that seemed successful? If so, what made it that way? What is a "successful" church? What are you looking for in a church?

Read: Acts 4:32-37

Reflect: Some people today are "church hoppers." They keep changing churches in search of the perfect one. The problem is they'll never be fully satisfied, because there is no perfect church. Anytime you have a group of people getting together, even Christians, there are issues and problems. I find it funny that the churches I've attended always seem better to me after I've left!

But that doesn't mean we should give up on the church. Maybe it just means we should restore the original settings from time to time, as we do with a computer that's gummed up. So let's see if we can identify some of the distinctive characteristics of this first-century church.

The first thing we notice is they were unified, "one in heart and mind" (4:32). That sounds really good, but what could it mean? This passage doesn't unpack it for us, but we've picked up several clues already in Acts. The church worshiped and prayed together; they made following Jesus their top priority; they relied on God's power, not their own. That's a pretty good foundation for any church.

Next, our passage introduces us to another important characteristic of the first church: radical sharing. Some readers may see in this a kind of Christian socialism, but we should be careful not to apply modern labels too quickly to biblical situations. The fact is, what motivated these followers of Jesus to let go of their resources was not their commitment to a political agenda. Rather, it was their commitment to God. They had an uncommon trust in God's sovereignty and ability to provide for them. How does your church express its trust in God?

The believers' willingness to give sacrificially was not just a passing fancy for wealth redistribution. They were reflecting God's concern for the poor and needy (see Psalm 140:12; Proverbs 31:9). Regardless of how we do it today, or even how much we give, all Christians need to care about "the least of these" (Matthew 25:40), because God does. Notice too the absence of pressure in their giving. We see this in the example of Barnabas; he gives with no strings attached. He simply places his major gift "at the apostles' feet" (Acts 4:36-37). Nice.

True, this may not have been the perfect church, but these Christians had the big things right, and they were making a difference in their world—or as Luke comments, "much grace was upon them all" (4:33). God blesses a church that operates like this.

Apply: Think of some ways you could make a sacrificial gift this week, whether financially or in some other way. Pray about your ideas, select one, and do it.

DISCUSSION QUESTIONS

After you've completed the five readings in the section "The Church Begins to Grow," get together with another person or group to talk about the things you've learned. Begin by sharing the insights you've gained from your own reflection on the passages. Then use the following questions to help you continue the conversation.

1. Has God ever healed you, or someone close to you? Explain what happened. How did it affect your faith? (Acts 3:1-10)

2. How do you feel about discussing spiritual things with people you don't know? Have you ever had an opportunity to do so, and what happened? (Acts 3:1-10)

3. Do you think most Christians are effective in the way they talk about Jesus with nonbelievers? What are some things you've learned about how to speak effectively? (Acts 3:11-26)

4. Are you certain that Jesus is coming back someday? How does that affect your life today? How would you explain your belief in the second coming of Jesus to a nonbelieving friend? (Acts 3:11-26)

5. Is it offensive or wrong to say that Jesus is the only way to heaven? (Acts 4:1-22)

6. What would you say is the difference between tolerating someone's beliefs and respecting them as a person? Why does this matter when you have spiritual conversations? (Acts 4:1-22)

7. Share an example of when you did something that was spiritually bold. Why did you do it, and what happened? (Acts 4:23-31)

8. How would you describe the difference between spiritual bravado and spiritual boldness? Can you point to some examples? (Acts 4:23-31)

9. What is your definition of a healthy church? What could you do to influence your church in this direction? (Acts 4:32-37)

10. Why is it so important for our witness for Christ to balance spiritual and social concerns? How could you achieve such a balance in your life and ministry? (Acts 4:32-37)

[WEEK THREE]

The Church Is Persecuted

Given its dramatic birth and rapid growth, it was only a matter of time before the first-century church began to attract criticism. The famous circus leader P. T. Barnum is reported to have said, "I don't care what they say about me in the newspaper, so long as they spell my name right." Yet what we discover in our next five readings is that the opposition to the early church was far more than negative public relations. It was the first outpouring of what has become more than two thousand years of persecution.

It's important to recognize that it wasn't just nonbelievers who caused trouble for the church. Even church insiders like Ananias and Sapphira disrupted the work of the kingdom. Later, the church would be infected by many false teachers. These cases underscore the need for loving accountability no matter what role we have in Christian mission. Our other readings give us pictures of more familiar kinds of persecution from those who resent or reject the gospel—imprisonment, flogging and, in the case of Stephen, martyrdom.

A popular bumper sticker today proclaims the utopian dream of religious pluralism: *Coexist*. No harm in that. But I often sense the unspoken message of those who display it is that Christians are the most intolerant toward such a peaceful vision. However, history shows the reverse; Christians are among the most persecuted people on earth and they've been experiencing persecution in various forms since Jesus returned to heaven, as we'll see in our next readings.

The writer of Hebrews lists examples of what early Christians faced (Hebrews 11:32-40), but there are plenty more stories. The classic *Foxe's Book of Martyrs* (published in 1563) and the more contemporary *Jesus Freaks* (published in 1999) document just a fraction of persecution cases throughout history. Even our current daily news contains examples of church burnings and death threats against Christians in various parts of the world. Unfortunately, persecution is something the church will have to endure until Jesus returns.

Why is it that in every age there are people who have a vendetta against the church? Some of it can be attributed to political or ideological struggles. But ultimately the reason the church has faced opposition since its earliest days is spiritual. As the apostle Paul said in his letter to the church in Ephesus, "For our struggle is not against flesh and blood, but against the rulers, against the authorities, against the powers of this dark world and against the spiritual forces of evil in the heavenly realms" (Ephesians 6:12).

So let's take a look at the struggles and courage of the early Christians and see how their example can guide us in our efforts to serve God today.

DAY ELEVEN: Lying to God

Prepare: Spend a few minutes thanking God for the ways he's blessed you in your life. What things are you most grateful for?

Read: Acts 5:1-16

Reflect: Over the years I've been asked many times to make "the pitch" at fundraising banquets. I usually begin by saying, "Well, we've had a

great evening so far, but now it's time for the Sermon on the *Amount*."
It always gets a chuckle and lightens the mood for my request. That's
not what happened in this passage. After the news about Ananias and
Sapphira spread, no one was laughing (5:11).

But aside from the sensational aspect of this account, our current
passage gives us a glimpse into a reality of the early church that we
have not yet seen. Satan was at work in the midst of the incredible
birth and growth of the church (5:3). This story is a reminder that even
when God is on the move, and even when we are clearly making a
difference for him, we are vulnerable to the strategies of the enemy
and we need to be on our guard (1 Peter 5:8-9). So what temptations
led to the downfall of this "major donor" church couple?

First, they cared more about image than reality. Ananias was trying
to act like he was making an all-out sacrificial gift when in fact he was
protecting his own bank account. He wanted to look like Barnabas
(Acts 4:36-37) while acting like Judas (John 12:4-6). As Peter pointed
out, the issue wasn't the size of the gift. Rather, it was Ananias's pre-
meditated attempt to appear to be someone he wasn't. That's lying to
God (Acts 5:4).

Second, Ananias and Sapphira loved money and possessions. There
is nothing inherently wrong with money. We need it to live. But it is
an incredibly powerful temptation (1 Timothy 6:10). Why? Because it
draws out of the human heart the desire for power and happiness on
our own terms instead of God's. The discipline of sacrificial giving
helps protect us from the love of money and keeps our hearts free and
open for God's leading.

The silver lining to this tragedy is that it seems to have produced a
healthy fear of God in the church (5:5, 11). I was once in a Bible study
with a man who had a big problem with the concept of fear of God.
For him it conjured up an image of a mean, angry deity that required
humans to cower. *Fear God . . . or else!* But a biblical understanding has
more to do with respect, awe, obedience and love for the maker of

heaven and earth. That's what the experience regarding Ananias and Sapphira produced in these early believers, and it led to a new season of growth and ministry in the church (5:12-16).

Apply: Think of something other than money you could give to someone who needs it. Then offer to give it away, no strings attached. Afterward, jot down how the experience made you feel about yourself and your walk with God.

DAY TWELVE: We're in the Jailhouse Now

Prepare: Reflect on some times in your life when you've experienced criticism or even ridicule for being a Christian. What did you learn from those experiences, and how did they affect your faith?

Read: Acts 5:17-42

Reflect: I remember standing on a busy street corner in Philadelphia and watching in horror as a race riot almost broke out. A group of white men, who were clearly in the wrong, was taunting a group of black men to fight. Just as things were about to get violent, a slightly built white man in a suit and tie stepped between the two groups. He gently put his hand on the chest of the leader of the black men and said something I couldn't hear. With that, the men stopped, turned around and left without incident. The courageous man in a suit then disappeared into the crowd, but I've always wondered if he was an angel.

No doubt the apostles wondered what was going on that night in the jailhouse. But in this case, the Bible confirms it was an angel who sprung them loose and instructed them to "tell the people the full message of this new life" (5:20). They responded, *Yes, sir!* One of the strongest motivations for serving God occurs when our knowledge of him is ignited by an unexpected experience of him. Has that ever happened to you?

In some ways, it's not hard to understand the reaction of the religious leaders; after all, part of their job was to protect people from heresy. But their irritation was more than just a distaste for proselytizing. What fueled the Sadducees' rage was their jealousy (5:17). In Israel at that time, the high priest was "the man," and together with the Sadducees, Pharisees and teachers of the law, he called the shots. The real problem was that these followers of Jesus were taking away the one thing the religious leaders wanted most: control.

Dictators of every age, whether political or religious, have become jealous, irrational and violent when Christians make clear they are under a higher authority (5:29). But we can take heart that opposition has never permanently stopped the growth of God's kingdom. In fact, it has only empowered the followers of Jesus and strengthened the church, as we see in this passage. Those who want to serve God today are likely to encounter opposition, though perhaps not as directly as these apostles did.

In the midst of this struggle, Gamaliel, who incidentally was the apostle Paul's original teacher (Acts 22:3), emerged as a voice of reason. He called for an executive session and attempted a little strategic "boardsmanship," advising his colleagues to take a wait-and-see approach (5:38-39). How many arguments in the church today could benefit from such advice? This passage reminds us not to be too quick to criticize the actions or methods of other Christians today. God may be at work in ways that we aren't recognizing.

Apply: What are some other "obey God rather than men" decisions in the Bible or church history? Do you face such a decision now? What do you sense God prompting you to do?

DAY THIRTEEN: Trouble in River City

Prepare: Spend a few minutes thanking God for the ministry opportunities he's given you in the past. Then spend time asking him to show you new ways you can serve him in the future.

Read: Acts 6:1-15

Reflect: In the hit Broadway musical *The Music Man*, con man Harold Hill famously used the line "Ya got trouble, right here in River City" to manufacture a problem. His goal was to swindle the people of River City into paying him lots of money to solve it. Anyone who's seen the play knows that his ploy didn't work out as planned; Harold falls in love and in the end does the right thing.

Unlike the musical, our current passage describes two very real sources of trouble in the early church, troubles that, left unaddressed, threatened to derail this growing movement of Christians. The first was *internal*: church members were arguing about the perceived fairness in the distribution of aid (6:1). One of the most discouraging things for Christian leaders is when those who want to make a difference for God get caught up in arguing about how to do it. It's a self-defeating waste of energy.

But like it or not, resolving conflict is part of doing ministry, and that's what makes these verses so instructive. Notice that the apostles' first response was to gather everyone together (6:2). Instead of allowing factions and gossip to take over, the Twelve dealt with the problem straight on with the whole group, just as they had seen Jesus do (see Matthew 20:24-28). Next, the leaders reminded everyone of their main objective. If the enemy can't prevent us from being involved in ministry, he can attempt to make us forget why we're doing it. That's why effective Christian leaders are good at keeping everyone focused on God's priorities. Finally, the solution to the problem was based on the conviction that administration was a spiritual task requiring highly qualified people for it to be done well (6:3, 6). As a result, the church continued its rapid growth (6:7). This is a reminder that effective ministry must value and utilize a full range of spiritual gifts (Romans 12:6-8).

The second source of trouble for the church at this moment was *external*: opposition from the religious establishment to Stephen, someone who had developed a particularly effective ministry (6:5, 8).

Some Christian leaders today use the media to attract opposition in an effort to get more attention for themselves and their organizations. But that's not Christlike ministry; it's spiritual showmanship. Luke makes clear that Stephen's motives and power were rooted in his faith and in the Holy Spirit (6:5, 8, 10), which is why Stephen is such a good model for those in ministry today. As for the opposition, they just couldn't get over their jealousy. They were the ones manufacturing "trouble" (6:11, 13), but unlike Harold Hill, they weren't open to learning any good lessons (Acts 5:33).

This passage reminds us that even when we are doing the right thing for God, in the right way, we're still going to face trouble and opposition. So rather than being surprised or derailed by it, we should prepare to handle it in the way that these early Christians did.

Apply: Can you think of an area of conflict or disagreement among Christians you know? What practical step could you take in the next week to help resolve it? Call or email someone? Invite someone to breakfast or to your home for dinner? What else?

DAY FOURTEEN: Good News for a Hostile World

Prepare: Take some time to reflect on your faith journey. What have been the high points in your relationship with God?

Read: Acts 7:1-19

Reflect: A few years ago I gave a talk about why Jesus is the only way to God. That really bothered a man in the audience and he kept interrupting and disagreeing with me throughout the session. "The Bible says we should love God and neighbor," he asserted, "but it never said *that*." After the meeting he continued the argument, so I respectfully pointed out that the uniqueness of Christ wasn't my idea. It's what Jesus said (John 14:6).

In this passage, Stephen had it a lot worse than I did in that session;

he was defending himself against an angry mob. How do you handle situations of confrontation or accusation? It helps to remember that sometimes the most heated arguments "over principle" are in fact disagreements about style or tradition, which seems to be the case here (Acts 6:11-14). But the problem was also more than that, as we've already seen. What really ticked off these religious leaders was that they were feeling threatened by and jealous of the apostles. That combination can make good people go ballistic.

So what was Stephen up to in this passage with his lesson about Abraham? In essence he was building a case for Christ by retracing the beginnings of Israel's history. What becomes clear is that God is the one who has been taking the initiative all along. It was God who chose Abraham and told him, "Go to the land I will show you" (Acts 7:3). It was God who promised to produce a great nation and a great blessing from Abraham (Genesis 12:1-3). And now, Stephen implies, it is God who has delivered that blessing through the birth, death and resurrection of Jesus of Nazareth. Stephen doesn't explicitly make that point just yet, but clearly that's where the puck is headed.

What can we learn from the first half of Stephen's speech? First, it's helpful to look back. The religious leaders were so angry that they had lost sight of God's big picture. When we experience disagreements with other believers today, it's a good idea to reflect together on the things we have in common, which are often far more significant than the cause of the conflict.

Second, it also helps to look back *with others*. The religious leaders knew the story of Abraham by heart, but they had missed the main point. Today, even committed followers of Christ can misinterpret what the Bible says, or misunderstand what God has been doing in their lives. That's why taking this journey through Acts with a group is so important. It gives us opportunities to receive loving and constructive input from other believers. Sadly, the religious leaders weren't willing to change their hearts or minds. Even so, Stephen's speech gives us a model for how to communicate the good news to a hostile world.

Apply: Who in your circle of influence would you say is hostile to the good news about Jesus? Pray for that person, and ask God to show you how you can be an effective witness.

DAY FIFTEEN: Courageous Evangelism

Prepare: Spend some time thanking God for the people you know, either personally or from history, who have sacrificed to enable you to know the good news about Jesus.

Read: Acts 7:20–8:1a

Reflect: Whenever I hear someone preach about Moses, I can't help thinking of Charlton Heston in the movie *The Ten Commandments*. Coming down from the mountain, he was all strong and righteous, holding up those stone tablets into the wind. For me, Moses is an Old Testament superhero. But in our current passage, Stephen adds some details that don't fit the Hollywood script: Moses was a kid from a broken home who went to a fancy boarding school, and had anger issues and a messiah complex (7:20-26). Complicated guy.

What was Stephen's point in rehashing the Moses story? He was using it to carefully inch toward a conclusion he knew his audience didn't want to hear. In addition to the realistic picture of Moses, notice how Stephen also highlighted the way the chosen people reacted to Moses, their divinely commissioned deliverer (7:35-36). Israel had a history of rejecting its saviors. *Hmmm.* Then Stephen quoted Moses himself predicting a prophet who was yet to come, a clear reference to the Messiah (7:37). This implies that preaching about Jesus Christ was not disrespecting Israel's history and religion, it was fulfilling it. *Now wait just a minute!*

I think something must have happened between verses 50 and 51. Maybe the crowd's body language showed they weren't listening. Or maybe one of the religious leaders booed or spoke out. We don't know. What we do know is that in verse 51, Stephen took off the gloves and let them have it.

This raises an interesting question: When, if ever, is it appropriate to verbally attack those who have different religious beliefs than ours? Since the church was born its history has been filled with arguing and division. I think the often-overlooked New Testament book of Jude gives us some helpful guidance. In writing about false teaching that was damaging the church, Jude counsels that we should "contend for the faith" with the false teachers, but "be merciful to those who doubt," that is, the average church member (Jude 1:3, 22). Perhaps the reason the church is so divided today is that we've reversed those two approaches.

In any case, Stephen concluded his sermon with a riff of point-blank accusations. *You're all a bunch of proud, Spirit-opposing, hypocritical murderers!* Makes for an awkward coffee hour. But it didn't really matter how he ended because this sermon was the last straw for a crowd that was already out to get him. Even as he died, Stephen continued to be a witness for Christ (7:55-56), which further infuriated his opponents.

Luke ends this story like a good movie director, giving us a quick glimpse of a new character (8:1), someone we'll be hearing much more about soon. But for now Luke lets us ponder the courage and impact of Stephen, a man full of faith and the Holy Spirit, who became the church's first martyr. Sadly, he wouldn't be the last.

Apply: Think of a person you know who is hostile to the Christian faith. On a piece of paper, make an outline of the way you'd make the case for Christ to that person. Now, pray that God would give you an opportunity to do so.

DISCUSSION QUESTIONS

After you've completed the five readings in the section "The Church Is Persecuted," get together with another person or group to talk about the things you've learned. Begin by sharing the insights you've gained from your own reflection on the passages. Then use the following questions to help you continue the conversation.

1. What are some ways you can make sure your inner life remains consistent with your outer life as a Christian? (Acts 5:1-16)

2. How do you feel about "the fear of God"? When is it a good thing and when is it harmful? (Acts 5:1-16)

3. Have you or a church you've been part of ever experienced persecution, whether great or small, for your commitment to Jesus Christ? How did you/they respond? (Acts 5:17-42)

4. Have you ever been in a situation where you felt you had to obey God rather than people? What happened? (Acts 5:17-42)

5. What are your spiritual gifts, and how do you use them? How might your church become more effective at using the spiritual gifts in the congregation? (Acts 6:1-15)

6. Think about some controversies in your church or within the wider Christian community. Do they seem more about principle and truth, or about style and tradition? How can you tell the difference? (Acts 6:1-15)

7. Who do you know, either personally or by reputation, that is most hostile to the gospel and teachings of God's Word? Why do you think they feel this way? (Acts 7:1-19)

8. What examples of church persecution do you know of today? What is the best way to respond to persecution? (Acts 7:1-19)

9. For you, what are the most significant high points in the Old

Testament, and how do they fit into God's plan of salvation? (Acts 7:20–8:1a)

10. What are the most significant high points in your life, and how did they lead you to a relationship with Jesus? (Acts 7:20–8:1a)

Part Two

THE ESSENTIAL MESSAGE

[WEEK FOUR]

The Good News Changes Lives

In our next five passages we'll read one of the greatest life-change stories in all of human history: the conversion of Saul (Paul). As a man who had built his career and reputation around an all-out effort to destroy the Christian church, Saul was a most unlikely convert. But the assumption that anyone is unsavable reveals a lack of understanding about the power of God's good news. History is filled with notable examples of people whose lives were transformed by the gospel, from St. Augustine, to Martin Luther, to C. S. Lewis, to Josh McDowell, to Joni Eareckson Tada and many others.

But it's not just famous people who demonstrate the power of God to change a life. In fact, the millions of ordinary men, women and children through the ages whose lives have been transformed by the good news make the case for the truth of the gospel even more powerfully. Even those skeptical about Christ must ask, "What accounts for the extraordinary ability of the Christian gospel to change lives?"

Our readings also guide us through what I call "The Philip Chapter." For the first half of Acts, Peter is the leading man. He's the one who "stands up" at key times to explain what God is doing, to call people to action and to defend the fledgling church. In the second half of Acts, Paul becomes the focal point as we follow him on several church-planting journeys. Of course the real star is God the Holy Spirit, who was poured out on the Day of Pentecost and who actively influences people and events throughout the entire book.

But in chapter 8 the spotlight is on Philip. While he may not be the leading man in Acts, he still had a powerful ministry in the early church because of his thorough knowledge of the Scriptures and his ability to recognize and obey the promptings of God. Those are spiritual skills anyone in ministry needs to cultivate.

In the end, what Peter, Saul and Philip had in common is that they all had encounters with Jesus, and that's what changed their lives. Meeting Jesus still transforms people today. At some point, every person must answer the question Jesus himself asked: "Who do you say I am?" (Matthew 16:15-16).

DAY SIXTEEN: The B-List Apostle

Prepare: Think of a time when you faced difficulties or disasters in your life. What did you learn about God from the experience?

Read: Acts 8:1b-25

Reflect: In this reading we come to another turning point in the book of Acts: widespread persecution. So far we've seen increasing resistance to the growth of the church, but after Stephen's martyrdom "a great persecution" broke out (8:1). Luke even introduces a kind of Darth Vader character into his narrative: *Saul, the destroyer of the church* (8:3).

But as we soon find out, God was planning to use what seemed like a disaster to accomplish a bigger plan. The persecution scattered the believers, so the good news began to spread, like dandelion seeds blown by the wind. It's helpful when we face difficulties and disasters in our lives today to remember that God can still use them to accomplish things we can't imagine. Sometimes we can only see what God is up to by looking back.

Imagine how perplexed the apostles must have been with God's plan. Jesus spent three years convincing them he was the promised Messiah, but God let him get crucified. Jesus miraculously came back to life, but God took him away after only a few weeks. The Spirit was poured out and the church began to grow, but God let the religious establishment bust it apart before it got going. What kind of plan is that?

What the apostles couldn't fully see is that God's plan wasn't to make one local church; instead he was building one universal church. Persecution was his way of turbocharging the spread of the good news to "the ends of the earth" (Acts 1:8). Sometimes serving God requires us to let go of a good thing we have in order to receive a better thing *he* has.

The passage next zooms in on one of the scattered believers. I've always been intrigued by Philip. He wasn't a "franchise player" like Peter or John, who attracted all the attention. Even so, Philip was a gifted follower of Christ who had a strategic role in spreading the church to Samaria and Africa. Over and over again, the Bible shows us that God seems to prefer "B-list players," those who don't look like superstars, to do his work (Hebrews 11:32-40).

Simon the sorcerer totally missed that point. Although he seems to have made a genuine faith commitment (8:13), he longed for A-list status more than he sought a heart for God, and it prevented him from facing the sin patterns in his life (8:9, 23). Simon was initially drawn to Christ by signs and wonders, which God often uses to advance his kingdom. But he needed a solid grounding in God's Word and a Christian mentor to disciple him. Those are essential for anyone serving God today.

Apply: Jot down the names of three "B-list" followers of Christ that you know or know of—people who aren't in the spotlight but who faithfully and effectively serve God. Pray that God would bless them, and pray that God would help you follow their example.

DAY SEVENTEEN: Effective Evangelism

Prepare: What words come to your mind when you think of sharing your faith with others? Who first talked with you about Jesus? How did you feel about the conversation at the time? How do you feel about it now?

Read: Acts 8:26-40

Reflect: *I'm no Billy Graham. I'm uncomfortable talking about spiritual things with people I don't know.* A lot of people feel that way, including me sometimes. But in this passage God makes clear that this was exactly what he wanted Philip to do: share his faith with a stranger. Let's examine how the story unfolds to see if we can learn some things about sharing the good news today.

First, notice that God created the opportunity for this spiritual conversation. Philip was just minding his own business when an angel and then the Spirit instructed him to meet and approach the Ethiopian official (8:26, 29). Our opportunities for faith sharing may not come from such dramatic interventions today, but if we learn to recognize the many ways God prompts us, we'll have more and more opportunities to naturally talk about spiritual things with others. Perhaps evangelism seems so unpleasant because often the emphasis is on a forced technique more than our ability to recognize a moment for sharing.

Second, notice the role of questions in this encounter. Philip asked, "Do you understand what you are reading" (8:30)? Brilliant! Simply asking questions and thoughtfully listening is an excellent, nonthreatening way to start a spiritual conversation. Philip's approach was like a Google search of the Ethiopian's questions. People today are on all sorts of spiritual journeys. Like Philip, we must be ready to come alongside and help them "hyperlink" to the answers about Jesus.

Finally, notice the importance of the Scriptures. The Ethiopian was intrigued by a passage from Isaiah (8:32-34). Obviously Philip was familiar with the passage, which no doubt means he had developed the practice of regularly reading God's Word himself. But the key wasn't his expertise in the prophetic writings. Rather it was his clear understanding of the Bible's greatest story, the story of Jesus (8:35). You may not know everything about the Bible; few people do. But being able to guide others through the biblical storyline of salvation is an essential ministry skill.

Philip wasn't one of the high-profile apostles in the early church, but he was an effective witness for his Lord nonetheless because he had the courage to act on God's promptings, and he had the conviction that God's Word had the power to change lives. Philip's example shows us that in the end, the Bible is its own best evangelist.

Apply: Spend some time on the Internet researching ministries that are engaged in Bible translation, distribution or engagement. Pray about whether and how God would have you get involved with one of them.

DAY EIGHTEEN: Seeing the Light

Prepare: What convinces you that Jesus is alive and that he wants to know you?

Read: Acts 9:1-9

Reflect: According to *The American Heritage Dictionary of Idioms*, the phrase "see the light" originated in the late 1600s and was used to indicate religious conversion. Maybe so. But I'd say we can make a stronger case that the phrase was inspired by Luke's description of what happened on the road to Damascus, probably around A.D. 33. Our current passage contains the ultimate example of seeing the light (9:3-6), which changed Saul's life and the world forever.

For me, this famous conversion account raises two challenging questions. First, why was Saul such an angry young man? The simple answer is, he didn't like Christians. To him they were traitors and heretics, so they needed to be stopped. But the rest of the story is more complex. On some level, Saul's anger was an expression of his passion for God, or at least his view of God. No doubt he was also defending his turf, that is, the nation of Israel and the temple. Or he could have been trying to earn the approval of his superiors, proving he was gung ho for God and ready for a big promotion.

But whatever the rationale, Luke wants to make sure we understand the vehemence of Saul's opposition to "the Way" (9:2), because it dramatically underscores the power of God to change lives. Only God could transform a person known for "breathing out murderous threats" against the followers of Christ (9:1) into the greatest Christian evangelist the world has ever known (9:20-22), and do it in a flash. Most conversions are not this dramatic. But whenever a person accepts Jesus Christ as Savior and Lord, it is no less miraculous. The convert is immediately transferred from what Saul later described as "the dominion of darkness" to "the kingdom of light" (Colossians 1:12-14)—and better than anyone else Saul would understand what that involved.

The second question that emerges from this passage is this: Why did God choose Saul for such a divine intervention in the first place? Weren't there others around who were more acceptable, or at least less volatile? Probably. But again, God's choice underscores the miracle of salvation. The point is, Saul didn't deserve it, but God saved him anyway. As a result, Saul became a living definition of God's grace. As Saul later wrote, "For it is by grace you have been saved, through faith—and this not from yourselves, it is the gift of God—not by works, so that no one can boast" (Ephesians 2:8-9).

The fact is, we don't fully know why God chose Saul. Or why he chose any of us, for that matter. All we know is that he did, and we should be eternally thankful. Through Saul's unlikely conversion, God communicated some essential truths about the nature of his good news, truths he went to great lengths to ensure that his church, and the world, would never forget.

Apply: In what way are you "a living definition of grace"? Jot down your answer and then decide if you'd like to share it with a Christian friend or family member.

DAY NINETEEN: I Want You!

Prepare: Have you ever sensed God nudging you to do something that seemed odd, embarrassing or even a little risky? How did you respond, and what was the result?

Read: Acts 9:10-19a

Reflect: Do you remember those old US Army recruiting posters where a determined Uncle Sam is pointing straight ahead and saying, "I want you!"? Ananias must have felt singled out after awakening from his vision—only the one doing the pointing was God, and the poster had his name on it: "Ananias!" (9:10).

How does God call people today? Sometimes it can be the result of a dramatic experience, like Ananias had. But other times it can come from reading Scripture, praying or receiving wise counsel from other Christians, all of which are ways we can hear the "still small voice" of God's guidance (1 Kings 19:12 KJV).

But regardless of how the call comes, the most important thing is how we respond. Ananias's simple "Yes, Lord" (Acts 9:10) is a model for us today. It echoes Samuel's response many centuries earlier, "Speak,

LORD, for your servant is listening" (1 Samuel 3:9, 10). When we sense God leading, our first response should be that of a good soldier, "Yes, sir! Reporting for duty, sir!"

That's not to say we'll always understand everything God has in mind. In fact, in spite of his initial response Ananias was clearly nervous about what God had asked him to do (Acts 9:13-14); perhaps he even had some reluctance to reach out to an archenemy of the church. Do you ever feel afraid or reluctant to reach out to people in your world? Or maybe Ananias thought Saul's conversion was a trick. *Are you sure you know what you're doing, God?*

I sense some impatience in God's response: "Go!" (9:15). There's a time for questions, but there's also a time to get moving (see Exodus 14:15). When waiting on the Lord becomes delaying on the Lord, there's a problem. God had a mission for Ananias. It wasn't to change the world; it was to reach out to one person, and that was a vital part of God's plan. Imagine how different the church and the world would be today if Ananias had refused to reach out to Saul. If we want to make a difference for God, we must trust that he has a plan, even when we don't understand it, and even when it's different from our own.

Where was Saul during this dialogue between Ananias and God? He was fasting and praying (9:9, 11). God had rocked Saul's world, and he needed time to rethink his assumptions and direction in life. Have you ever had that kind of life-changing experience? Our passage doesn't make a big deal of it, but it's significant that Saul was baptized (9:18); the former destroyer of the church was now publicly identified as one of them. What we learn from Ananias and Saul is that God can do incredible things through people who are willing to say, "Yes, sir" when he calls.

Apply: Over the past year, has there been something you've sensed God wants you to do, big or small? What would it mean for you to say, "Yes, sir!" to that leading? Record your response in the Essential Question Journal.

DAY TWENTY: Spiritual Mentor

Prepare: Who are your spiritual heroes from history and the present? What do you admire about these people? Are you a spiritual hero to someone?

Read: Acts 9:19b-31

Reflect: In 1938, a British schoolboy named John Stott accepted Jesus Christ as his Savior because of a talk given by a Scripture Union staff worker named Eric Nash (AKA, "Bash"). Stott went on to become one of the most influential biblical scholars, authors and evangelical leaders in the world until his death in 2011. But what many don't know is that for the five years following his conversion, Stott received a weekly letter from Bash, who took the time to help the new believer understand and grow in the faith.[1]

That's what Barnabas did for Saul: he befriended and defended him (9:27-28). Imagine how different the world might be today if Barnabas had left Saul on his own. We'll never know for sure, but Barnabas's willingness to advocate for a person no one else trusted was a critical factor in the growth of the church. Barnabas demonstrated that the long-term impact of a spiritual mentor to new believers, especially those recovering from a major failure in life, is incalculable.

It's interesting that Saul wasted no time sharing his newfound faith. "*At once* he began to preach" (9:20). He didn't calculate what his conversion might do to his reputation, his friends, his career or anything else. Saul knew that if Jesus is alive, everything else is secondary. Having that sense of priority in life is the engine that drives our effectiveness for God.

But Saul wasn't the only one who had undergone a transition. The religious leaders were used to being respected and honored in the community. Now momentum had definitely turned against them. First, they lost one of their star players (9:21). Next, they were beaten in public debate (9:22, 29). Finally, their opposition, the church, was growing. Literally in a flash, the Jewish chiefs in Damascus had gone from religious leaders to religious losers, and they were obsessed with striking back (9:23-24).

I wonder if Saul had a sense of buyer's remorse as he made his getaway in that basket (9:25). Oh sure, what happened on the Damascus Road was a life-changing experience. But now former colleagues hated him and his new "friends" were fearful and distrustful of him. We need to remember that conversion isn't the endgame of ministry. New Christians need extra care and encouragement to keep them from turning back. Saying "yes" to Jesus can happen in a moment, but learning how to be his follower takes a lifetime of discipleship.

Apply: Is there a new Christian you know, one who still has a lot of rough edges, who needs a faithful friend? What would it take for you to become a spiritual mentor?

DISCUSSION QUESTIONS

After you've completed the five readings in the section "The Good News Changes Lives," get together with another person or group to talk about the things you've learned. Begin by sharing the insights you've gained from your own reflection on the passages. Then use the following questions to help you continue the conversation.

1. When have you experienced a ministry or personal disaster? What did you learn about yourself and about God from the experience? (Acts 8:1b-25)

2. Simon the sorcerer was like a lot of people today: he wanted to seem spiritual. What's the difference between genuine faith and being seen as spiritual? (Acts 8:1b-25)

3. Have you ever had a faith-based conversation with a stranger? What happened and what did you learn about sharing the good news? In what ways has God led or prompted you in your life? (Acts 8:26-40)

4. Research shows that Bible reading is consistently declining, even in the church. Why do you think this is so? What helps you read and understand the Bible? (Acts 8:26-40)

5. Was there ever a time in your life when you were angry at God or the church? Talk about it. How have you been able to resolve the underlying issues? (Acts 9:1-9)

6. Describe your own conversion experience. Was it sudden, more of a long-term process, or are you still trying to figure it out? Where are you in your journey with Jesus? (Acts 9:1-9)

7. Who have been the most helpful spiritual mentors to you? Why? What would you say are the qualities of a good spiritual mentor? (Acts 9:10-19a)

8. How has the good news changed your life? (Acts 9:10-19a)

9. Are there people who have rejected or opposed you because of your Christian faith? What happened? (Acts 9:19b-31)

10. What do you think is the most effective response to being rejected for being a follower of Jesus? Share some examples. (Acts 9:19b-31)

[WEEK FIVE]

The Good News Is for Everyone

The main event in this section is a simple meeting between Peter and a man named Cornelius. Sounds pretty routine, but as you are about to discover, this meeting got a lot of ink in Acts and became one of the most significant turning points in the history of the church.

To understand what made the meeting so momentous, we need some background. Peter was a Jewish Christian while Cornelius was a Gentile, that is, a non-Israelite. Over the centuries the Jews had developed a deep animosity toward the Gentiles and saw it as an issue of personal holiness to avoid any contact with them whatsoever. So when the church began to spread among Jews of the first century, it inevitably raised the controversial question: Did God's plan of salvation include the Jews only, or was the good news of Jesus Christ for everyone, even the Gentiles?

This Jew-Gentile tension had become so deeply embedded by the first century that it took several dramatic interventions by God to overcome it. By the end of the meeting between Peter and Cornelius, God had emphatically answered the big question of the day: Yes, God wanted to save the Gentiles too. Actually, this all-inclusive vision had been God's intent from the very beginning (Genesis 12:1-3); it's just that his people had somehow missed the point. So the historic meeting of Peter and Cornelius was God's course correction for those who had drifted from his will.

Our next five readings also mark the end of a major phase in the church's early history. For the first several chapters in Acts, Peter was front and center, standing up to explain things and initiate the action when others were hesitant. Luke then followed the exploits of some of the other disciples, like Stephen and Philip, but for a long time Peter was the leading man. That would soon change, as these next passages are Peter's swan song; from Acts 13 on, it's all about Paul and his companions.

So let's give thanks for Peter. It's true he had some rough edges and made some mistakes. But from the day he left his nets to follow Jesus (Luke 5:1-11), Peter had developed a knack for reaching the "aha" moment before anyone else. He was the first disciple to recognize Jesus as the Christ (Matthew 16:15-16), he was the first believer to explain that God had sent the Holy Spirit (Acts 2:14-21), and he was the first church leader to realize that the good news was for everyone (Acts 10:43). Peter's unique ability to understand the purposes of God has defined the church ever since. Not bad for a lowly fisherman.

DAY TWENTY-ONE: Bold Humility

Prepare: Begin your quiet time with some breathing prayer. Breathe out worries and cares. Breathe in thanks and praise. Repeat.

Read: Acts 9:32-43

Reflect: Over the years I've enjoyed reading historical novels such as James Michener's *Chesapeake*. Each chapter tells the story of a different character and by the end all the stories weave together into one big narrative. That's a little like what Luke does in Acts. So far he's told the stories of Peter, John, Stephen, Philip and Paul. Together they give us a picture of how the first church grew. It makes for a good read, but we need to remember, Acts is history, not a novel.

In this reading we pick up Peter's story again, and the dominant theme is healing. Some are uncomfortable with this aspect of the Christian experience. Perhaps that's due to the way healing is presented in the media, or the way some televangelists seem to sensationalize it. But the obvious point of Luke's account is this: healing happens, so we shouldn't dismiss it because of the excesses.

Note that there doesn't seem to be some kind of magic formula to healing. With Aeneas, Peter appealed to Jesus Christ (9:34). With Dorcas (Tabitha), Peter prayed, then issued a direct command (9:40). The thing these healings have in common is they both had the same effect: "many people believed in the Lord" (9:35, 42). We should be skeptical of any healing ministry today that puts too much attention on the human vehicle. Healing should turn people to God.

With this in mind, put yourself in Peter's shoes here. What do you think he was feeling prior to each of these healings? The situation with Aeneas may have seemed familiar (see Acts 3:1-10); restoring a paralytic was a "normal" healing. But imagine how he felt when the messengers asked him to bring a dead woman back to life. *Is this really possible? Am I going to disappoint these good people and embarrass myself?* We don't know exactly what he thought or felt, but we do know he took it all to God in prayer (9:40). When Peter said amen he was ready to take a bold step of faith: "Tabitha, get up."

If you want to make a difference for God today, there are times when you must take the risk of prayerfully stepping into a challenging, even impossible situation. Peter gives us an example of the kind of bold humility God blesses.

Apply: What is the most challenging situation you are facing today? Spend some time praying about it, asking God for direction and for a sense of bold humility.

DAY TWENTY-TWO: The Divine Choreographer

Prepare: Reflect on the ways that God has intervened in your life. How have you responded to him?

Read: Acts 10:1-48

Reflect: It's difficult for us in the twenty-first century to appreciate what a big deal this meeting between Peter and Cornelius really was. Even though God's original plan was to bless the whole world through his chosen people (Genesis 12:1-3), by the first century Jews had developed strong hostility toward Gentiles and viewed them as outside God's plan of salvation. In fact, good Jews weren't supposed to visit, much less eat with, Gentiles. So when Peter went to Cornelius's house, he was breaking religious tradition, big time.

At first glance it might seem as though Cornelius's angelic vision came out of the blue, but the fact is, he had been seeking God for a long time. Luke tells us that Cornelius was God fearing, generous and prayerful (Acts 10:2); in other words, even as a Gentile he was living what author Leighton Ford calls "the attentive life,"[1] and that's what prepared him for this encounter with God. How encouraging to know that God is aware of our prayers and acts of service (Acts 10:4), and that "he rewards those who earnestly seek him" (Hebrews 11:6).

Meanwhile, Peter was having his own divine encounter, though it was physical hunger that particularly prepared him to hear God's voice this time. "Kill and eat" (Acts 10:13) is a jarring statement, especially for politically correct modern ears. But God was being direct because he wanted no misunderstanding. Over the centuries, human rules and traditions had obscured his saving purpose. So at this formative stage of the church, God stepped in to make a course correction. The good news, and therefore the church, was for everyone. As the apostle Paul later wrote, "So in Christ Jesus you are all children of God through faith, for all of you who were baptized into Christ have clothed yourselves with Christ. There is neither Jew nor Gentile . . . for you are all one in Christ Jesus" (Galatians 3:26-28 NIV 2011).

Maybe the Jew-Gentile tension is not as active today, but are there individuals or groups of people you can't imagine coming to genuine faith in Christ? *If we let them in, it'll ruin the church.* But the flaw in that attitude is this: keeping people out is what ruins the church. When Peter finally had his moment of realization (10:34-38), he understood the scope of God's good news: "everyone who believes in him (Jesus) receives forgiveness of sins through his name" (10:43). The chapter ends with yet another outpouring of the Spirit (10:44-46) and reminds us that God, the Divine Choreographer, is the one who has been orchestrating his plan of salvation from the very beginning.

Apply: Make a list of individuals and groups of people that you have trouble imagining could ever come to faith in Christ. Now ask the Divine Choreographer to make them open to his plans for them.

DAY TWENTY-THREE: Holy Legalism

Prepare: Think about your early experience with the church. Did you find the church restrictive, affirming or what else? How has that affected you today?

Read: Acts 11:1-18

Reflect: This passage feels like a summer rerun on TV. *Change the channel, I already saw this one!* But we shouldn't skip over Peter's retelling of his vision and subsequent meeting with Cornelius too quickly because it was a major turning point for the church and, as we can now appreciate, for the world.

As we learned in our consideration of Acts 10, the Jews had a long-standing dislike for Gentiles. The origin of this conflict had its roots in a good command of God; his chosen people were to be separate from the evil ways of the nations (Leviticus 20:26). But over the centuries that holy motivation had been lost in a human system of laws and prejudice. If the good news was going to spread, God had to break through that system of hate. That's why he intervened in such a dramatic way.

The Jew-Gentile issue may not be such a tension today, but this passage is a warning to us of the dangers of "holy legalism" in the church—that is, following the letter of the law but not the spirit of it as well (see Matthew 9:13). When Christians seem more interested in their rules than in living out God's love and mercy, seekers and nonbelievers begin to see the church as a negative force. One of the biggest challenges the church has in an increasingly secularized world is learning how to effectively speak the truth in love (Ephesians 4:15).

It's also instructive to consider how the early church began to deal with this controversy. The Jewish Christians in Jerusalem made the mistake of criticizing Peter before they knew all the facts (11:2-3). Perhaps this was motivated by their commitment to obey God's Word, but even so, they would have done much better to start by asking questions. What's your first reaction to another Christian who expresses different views from yours?

The most amazing thing in this passage is the way Peter responded to his critics. Think about Peter for a minute; he was a shoot first, ask questions later kind of guy (see John 18:10). But here Peter didn't respond with anger or even by taking personal offense. Instead, he calmly explained what happened and concluded, "Who was I to think that I could oppose God?" (Acts 11:17). Peter's growing maturity shows that calmly focusing attention on what God has done can be a much more effective witness than fighting.

Apply: What groups of Christians, and non-Christians, make you angry? Why? What is one practical way you could apply Peter's example to these situations?

DAY TWENTY-FOUR: The Church Goes Viral

Prepare: "Praise the LORD, my soul, and forget not all his benefits" (Psalm 103:2). How has God been good to you this week?

Read: Acts 11:19-30

Reflect: A few years ago two nerdy-looking "scientists" combined Diet Coke and Mentos candy to cause an explosion of fizz and foam. The homemade video of their goofy experiments went viral on YouTube and reached millions of people overnight. You get the feeling at the beginning of this passage that the church is about to "go viral" as well. A plan of salvation that included everyone, combined with persecution, produced explosive growth and made the church a grass-roots phenomenon (11:19-21).

But the question on the minds of the leaders back in Jerusalem was this: Was the phenomenon legitimate, a fad or worse? It's important to be discerning about new experiences or teachings that become popular among Christians today, especially in a media-driven world; it's easy for new believers to be misled. As the apostle John counseled, "Do not believe every spirit, but test the spirits to see whether they are from God, because many false prophets have gone out into the world" (1 John 4:1). So at this formative stage of the church, the leaders made a wise move: they sent Barnabas, "a good man, full of the Holy Spirit and faith" (Acts 11:24), to check things out. What would it take for you to develop that kind of reputation?

As it turned out, Barnabas became a strategic player in the early church. Like an effective executive, he had the ability to do a situation analysis and affirm the strengths he found (11:22-24). But he didn't stop there. Barnabas instinctively knew good leadership would be required, so he recruited Saul and trained him for the task (11:25-26). As we've already seen, identifying and mentoring new leaders is one of the best ways to make a long-term impact for the kingdom. Notice, too, that instead of keeping power for himself, Barnabas was concerned to find the right person for the job. Maybe that's why Antioch became the first missionary-sending church and the place where followers of Jesus were first called Christians (11:26).

Our passage ends with a note of realism; a severe economic downturn was soon to hit the Roman world (11:27-30). The point is that the church's explosive growth occurred in the face of difficulty. We sometimes assume that for the good news to spread, the economy must be strong, the "right" candidates must be elected and society must welcome the efforts of the church. But that's not what we see in Acts or in the rest of history; from the very beginning the church has experienced its greatest growth in the tough times. Instead of complaining or being immobilized, Christians should view hardships as an opportunity for growth. That's the beauty of an idea that goes viral; even without great resources or big sponsors, nothing can stop it.

Apply: What are some specific steps you could take to become more like Barnabas, "a good [person], full of the Holy Spirit and faith"? Ask for God's help in taking the first step this week.

DAY TWENTY-FIVE: The Unstoppable Force

Prepare: Pray this psalm: "For God alone my soul waits in silence; from him comes my salvation. He alone is my rock and my salvation, my fortress; I shall not be greatly shaken" (Psalm 62:1-2 ESV).

Read: Acts 12:1-25

Reflect: It's kind of confusing to keep track of all the Herods in the Bible. That's because "Herod" was the name of a royal family, with different members showing up at different points in the New Testament. For example, Herod the Great was the ruthless king that ordered the slaughter of all baby boys under the age of two around the time of Jesus' birth. Later, in Acts 25-26, we'll read about Herod Agrippa II, the king Paul attempted to convert in public. But the antagonist in this passage is Herod Julius Agrippa, or Agrippa I for short, a man willing to commit murder for political gain (12:2) and whose undoing was his out-of-control pride (12:21-23).

The question is, why did Luke include these unsavory details about this particular Roman king? The clue comes near the end of the chapter: "but the word of God continued to increase and spread" (12:24). Luke's point is that in spite of all the power, intrigue and evils of Rome, God's purposes could not be stopped. The same is true today. You may feel at the mercy of "the powers that be" (Romans 13:1 KJV) in your efforts to serve God, but the bigger truth is, "greater is he that is in you, than he that is in the world" (1 John 4:4 KJV). That's the source of our confidence.

Even so, Peter might have felt hopeless sitting in jail. *They took down John the Baptist, Jesus, Stephen, James, and I know I'm next.* But God had more for Peter to do and was about to release him for it in the most amazing way. Christians always have real hope, no matter the circumstances, because God is in charge.

The particulars of Peter's escape may seem like something out of an Indiana Jones movie—iron gates open by themselves, sixteen guards all sleep while the hero tiptoes past, with an angel leading the way. Peter even adds the comic relief: "*Now* I know without a doubt that the Lord sent his angel and rescued me" (12:11). I guess so! But this is no screenplay; it's Luke's detailed account of how the church was born and began to grow against all odds. As Jesus himself said, "What is impossible with men is possible with God" (Luke 18:27).

The most important part of the story is what was happening off stage: the church was praying for Peter (12:12). It's easy to overlook this aspect of ministry, especially when we are barely keeping up with all our urgent priorities. But skipping prayer disconnects us from the true source of our effectiveness and weakens our efforts to serve God. Over the centuries, the church has prevailed against the Herods of this world not by being strong and political, but rather by being weak and prayerful. That's what makes the good news an unstoppable force.

Apply: Make a list of some ways "the Herods" in your world are opposing the purposes of God. Pray now about these situations. Also, sometime in the next week, pray with other believers about them.

DISCUSSION QUESTIONS

After you've completed the five readings in the section "The Good News Is for Everyone," get together with another person or group to talk about the things you've learned. Begin by sharing the insights you've gained from your own reflection on the passages. Then use the following questions to help you continue the conversation.

1. What do you think about healing today? Does it still happen? How can we know if a healing ministry is legitimate, that is, truly of God? (Acts 9:32-43)

2. Can you share any experiences of God's healing in your life or those around you? What did you learn? (Acts 9:32-43)

3. Why do you think God heals some people, but not others? How should we respond when God doesn't seem to answer our prayers the way we want? (Acts 9:32-43)

4. Do you think prejudice hinders the spread of the gospel today? If so, how? (Acts 10–11)

5. Are there individuals or groups of people in the world today that seem outside of God's plan of salvation? Who, and why do you think this? (Acts 10–11)

6. Who are the unreached people groups in your world, and what could you do to reach out with the good news to them? (Acts 10–11)

7. What would you say is the most controversial issue in the church today? How are Christians engaging in the debate over it? What lessons from the way the first-century church handled the Jew-Gentile issue might apply? (Acts 10–11)

8. Have you ever experienced opposition when trying to serve God? What happened and what did you learn? (Acts 12:1-25)

9. Can you think of other world leaders in history who have opposed the gospel or persecuted Christians? What do we learn from history? (Acts 12:1-25)

10. What inspires and challenges you most about the life and ministry of Peter?

Part Three

THE ESSENTIAL MISSION

[WEEK SIX]

The First Mission Trip

In our next five readings we'll join Paul, Barnabas and several others on the first of three missionary journeys throughout the Roman Empire. In fact, these mission trips of Paul become the main focus for the rest of Acts, and, as you'll see, it's an exciting ride.

The starting point is a unique church in Antioch, the place where the disciples of Jesus were first called Christians (Acts 11:26). What made this church stand out was their *vision*. They believed the gospel could spread to everyone in the world. At the heart of their strategy, however, was not a long-range plan or a fundraising campaign. Those things have their place, but the church in Antioch developed their sense of vision through worship, prayer and fasting (Acts 13:1-3). Perhaps churches today would grow more effectively if they began their strategies in the way the church at Antioch did.

One theme to watch out for on this first mission trip is the difference between success and failure in ministry. At times many people responded to the good news; at other times the team met stiff resistance and had to retreat. Maybe the clearest example was in the town of Lystra. Initially the townsfolk were so impressed by the combination of a miraculous healing and powerful preaching that they cheered Paul and Barnabas as Zeus and Hermes in human form. Soon after, however, the crowd changed their minds and tried to kill the apostles. We see this success/failure overlap throughout the mission trips in Acts, and it reminds us to be ready for similar challenges today.

Another theme to keep an eye on is the way disagreements were settled. As we've already seen, the big issue for the early Christians was whether the Gentiles could really be part of the church. It all came to a head at the Council at Jerusalem, where the participants worked out a compromise that seemed to settle the issue, at least temporarily. Take note of the way the leaders developed a solution, because it offers us several principles that apply to similar situations today.

The readings end, however, with a reminder that even the greatest spiritual heroes have their moments of weakness. Paul and Barnabas, two men who had accomplished so much for God together, had a "sharp disagreement" and split up. As we'll see, it didn't thwart God's mission, but it is a case study of why worship, prayer and fasting are needed throughout a mission, not just at the beginning.

DAY TWENTY-SIX: A Mission from God

Prepare: What do you like and dislike about traveling? What's the longest or most difficult journey you've ever taken? Have you ever taken a mission trip? What was that like for you?

Read: Acts 13:1-12

Reflect: *The Blues Brothers* was a 1980 movie about two incorrigible young men who went on a concert tour to save a struggling orphanage. Along the way the boys got into trouble and ended up being chased by just about everyone in Chicago. The movie's poster captured the most famous line from the script, "They'll never get caught. *They're on a mission from God.*"

As it turns out, that's the theme of this passage too—Barnabas and Saul set out on a mission from God. Only this is no comedy; it's the first of three daring missionary journeys that resulted in the unprecedented growth of the church. But how do we know the difference between a genuine mission from God and a self-deluded claim of divine guidance? Our passage offers several principles that can help us with that question today.

First, Barnabas and Paul (Luke no longer uses the Jewish name Saul; 13:9) prepared themselves by waiting, worshiping and fasting (13:2). This would boil off any impure motivations. How do you prepare for a time of ministry? Second, the worshiping community, not just one person, sensed the direction of the Holy Spirit (13:1). We should be skeptical of those who claim a mission from God without spiritual accountability. Finally, Barnabas and Paul were commissioned by the church (13:3). That would make ongoing support possible. Prayer, fasting and a worshiping community were the ingredients that enabled them to discern this genuine mission from God.

I wonder how Barnabas and Paul felt as they walked into Salamis, the first city on their missionary tour. Perhaps they took a deep breath, looked each other in the eyes and said, "Let's roll." What happened next must have been a surprise: they encountered resistance that threatened to derail the mission from the very start (13:6-12). In an odd way, it was another proof of a genuine mission from God. We must be careful not to attribute every problem to spiritual opposition, especially problems of our own making, but anyone truly on a mission from God can expect pushback in some way.

Paul saw the situation for what it was. Elymas was not just being a pain in the neck; he was forwarding the agenda of the devil (13:10). The punishment for Elymas—temporary blindness—must have given

Paul a flashback to his own conversion experience. Behind Paul's stern words may have been a restorative motive. Sometimes the most loving thing God can do is stop us in our tracks. Paul would have known from experience how difficult it is to see the light until you understand how blind you really are.

Apply: Is there a mission, whether great or small, God has been nudging you to attempt? Write it down in the Essential Question Journal. Pray about it each time you read the Bible for the next few weeks.

DAY TWENTY-SEVEN: Pioneering Ministry

Prepare: Spend a few minutes asking God to speak to you from his Word today. Begin your prayer by saying, "Speak, Lord, for your servant is listening" (1 Samuel 3:9).

Read: Acts 13:13-52

Reflect: The most effective sermon I ever heard was also the shortest. It was at a mission conference and the preacher was Eric Frykenberg, a distant relative of mine. The speaker before him had gone way over time, so when Eric took the pulpit, he held up his notes and said, "There's not time for this now." Everyone breathed a sigh of relief. "But there's one thing I want to say," he continued. "The worst thing that's happened in my missionary career is when this old heart has gotten calloused. Don't let that happen to you." With that he bowed his head, overcome by emotion, and closed in prayer.

So far in Acts we've heard sermons from some of the greatest preachers in the early church: Peter in chapter 2, and Stephen in chapter 7. Now it's Paul's turn in the pulpit (13:16-41). We've already discovered what a powerful speaker he was, but the reaction to Paul's message at Pisidian Antioch was mixed. Some were drawn to it (13:42-43), while others opposed it (13:45, 50). But anyone who takes on the difficult task of pioneering ministry—that is, taking the good news where it has never been before—must be willing to persevere when ministry outcomes aren't easy to see or measure.

Our passage reveals another challenge of pioneering ministry, one that would intensify throughout Paul's missionary travels: jealousy. The religious officials were threatened by the growing popularity of the Christian movement, so they began mobilizing to stop it. Jesus had warned his followers this would happen (John 15:18-25). How ironic that Peter, John, Stephen and now Paul were all hated for spreading good news. That's why Paul wrote to the Ephesian Christians, "I pray that . . . he may strengthen you with power through his Spirit in your inner being" (Ephesians 3:16). Paul knew from experience that it takes a strong inner game to make a difference for God.

There's one more challenge Paul faced at this early stage of the journey, and it would be easy to overlook: a team member quit (13:13). Maybe John, whose full name was John Mark (Acts 15:37-38), was too young, or maybe he just couldn't handle the hardships of pioneering ministry. Some have speculated he was offended that his cousin, Barnabas, was no longer getting top billing. At the beginning of the mission, Luke referred to "Barnabas and Saul" (13:2), but by the time they reached Pisidian Antioch it had changed to "Paul and his companions" (13:13). We can't know for sure, but we do know that dissension within a mission team is as debilitating as opposition from without.

Our passage ends with a change in strategic plan; Paul turned his attention to the Gentiles, who proved to be a much more receptive audience (13:46-48). It was an example of what contemporary Christian author Henry Blackaby wrote, "When God reveals to you what He is doing around you, that is your invitation to join Him."[1]

Apply: Where would you say God is most at work in your life and ministry efforts? How could you more fully get involved in these opportunities?

DAY TWENTY-EIGHT: Successful Ministry

Prepare: What's the most successful ministry experience you've ever had? What's the most challenging ministry experience you've ever had? What did you learn from each?

Read: Acts 14:1-28

Reflect: When I was in college I had a summer job selling dictionaries door to door. I traveled around southern Virginia sharing my sales presentation hundreds of times, and I have to say it was tough work. People cursed and slammed the door in my face. A high-strung poodle bit me on the leg. The police hassled me, though I never broke the law. Even so, I earned more money selling books than all my other summer jobs combined.

I wonder if Paul and Barnabas ever felt like door-to-door salesmen. In Iconium, they made a great presentation and got positive results (14:1). But when things turned ugly they had to move on to a new sales territory (14:5-6). In Lystra, it looked like they made another big sale, but it was all undone by fierce competition, so they had to start over in Derbe (14:19-20). Maybe my summer job wasn't so bad after all.

But this passage raises an important question for those who want to make a difference for God today: Did Paul and Barnabas have a successful ministry? If by successful we mean organized, well-funded and without problems, then the answer is, no way! But if by successful we mean that people heard and believed the good news, and new churches were planted, then the answer is, absolutely! It reminds us that very often successful ministry is chaotic and messy by the world's standards. That's why Jesus challenged his followers to stay focused on the main thing: "go and bear fruit—fruit that will last" (John 15:16). That's the real definition of success.

These verses also contain one of the greatest examples of courage in the Bible. After the crowd in Lystra thought they had killed Paul and dragged his body out of the city (14:19), Paul got up and went right back in (14:20). I don't think I could do that. Then, he and Barnabas doubled back through all the towns where they had experienced trouble along the way (14:21-22). Sometimes successful ministry takes a lot of guts.

As this first missionary journey came to a close, we feel a sense of relief when Paul and Barnabas finally made it back to Antioch. But instead of hitting the talk show circuit, they immediately reported back to their sending church and highlighted how God had "opened the door of faith to the Gentiles" (14:27). That's because Paul and Barnabas were in it for God's glory, not theirs, all along.

Apply: Make a list of the most successful ministries and missionaries you know of. Pray for them and consider how you could support what they are doing.

DAY TWENTY-NINE: Ministry Disagreements

Prepare: Jesus prayed "for those who will believe in me . . . that all of them may be one, Father, just as you are in me and I am in you" (John 17:20-21). How could you be part of the answer to Jesus' prayer?

Read: Acts 15:1-21

Reflect: I was once on the board of a Christian organization that went through a split. The organization was facing a crisis and the board had some tough decisions to make. What made it so difficult is that everyone loved the Lord and wanted to do the right thing. But there were different opinions about what that meant. In the end, the two sides couldn't agree, and the board broke apart.

How should we resolve disagreements that inevitably emerge in the course of doing ministry? That's the big question underlying Acts 15. Unlike Paul and Barnabas's experience on their recent missionary journey, the opposition this time wasn't jealous religious leaders, intent on destroying the church. Instead, it was from *believers* who wanted to impose the law of Moses on the Gentiles as a condition of their salvation (15:1, 5). As we've discovered in our journey through Acts, that was the hot-potato issue for the first-century church. Let's unpack how they addressed it here and see if we can extract some principles that apply to ministry disagreements today.

Notice that the church's first move was to get all the players together to talk (15:2). Publicly criticizing people who hold different views may get "Amens" from those who already agree with us, but it only deepens the problem with those who don't. Second, the apostles and elders allowed everyone to express their views (15:4-7). Genuine listening by all sides is an essential ingredient in any solution. Third, the church evaluated the evidence presented by those directly involved, in this case Peter, Paul and Barnabas (15:6-12). Fourth, they looked to the Scriptures for guidance (15:15-18). That's our plumb line in any disagreement or decision. And finally, they accepted the decision of the leader (15:19-21).

But did it actually work? Did the "believers who belonged to the party of the Pharisees" (15:5) happily go along? It's not clear from this passage how the dissenters reacted; no doubt some were won over. But we know from other parts of the Bible that this issue didn't go away (see Galatians 3:1-25). It took a long time to work out. Even so, the experience of those involved in this Council at Jerusalem gives us a good model for today.

In my own painful experience, I discovered one other thing that made a difference. In the depths of our frustration, the entire board gathered in a little chapel for a service of repentance; we knelt down and asked for God's forgiveness. It took years for the board to recover from the disagreement, but I believe that moment in the chapel was the beginning of our healing process.

Apply: Is there a ministry disagreement that you know of, or are part of? What is one practical step you could take to be an influence for unity? Jot it down on a note card and keep it in your Bible until you've acted on it.

DAY THIRTY: Personal Disagreements

Prepare: Prepare your heart to hear God's word by saying the Lord's Prayer out loud, slowly and reflectively. "Our Father, who art in heaven, hallowed be thy name . . ."

Read: Acts 15:22-41

Reflect: Years ago I supervised the staff of a very effective ministry. Everyone was committed to reaching out with the gospel, but over time differing opinions developed about the best way to do that. This led to impassioned emails, difficult conversations and a growing level of distrust between the different sides. So I called a series of meetings in various locations to address the problem. I encouraged each person to speak his or her mind and I took notes on large sheets of paper taped to the walls. We also prayed together. From that we developed and circulated a document of shared principles for working together, and the ministry began moving forward again.

That's the basic storyline of this passage. The church leaders have "retreated" in Jerusalem, come to a compromise and are now sending a letter summarizing their agreement. Perhaps the key phrase is this: "It seemed good to the Holy Spirit and to us" (15:28). That captures the essence of their decision-making process and offers us a model for navigating difficult decisions today. Our first move must be to seek divine guidance through God's Word, prayer and fasting, but we must also use our God-given wisdom and common sense. Both approaches must come together to resolve disputes in a way that honors God and advances his purposes.

But what do we make of the letter's conclusion, asking Gentile believers to follow a few specific Jewish laws (15:29)? Doesn't that undermine the main point? Some have said yes, and view the agreement as flawed. But when we take the New Testament as a whole, we see that Paul never backed away from the principle that salvation was through Jesus Christ alone, with no preconditions or additives (Philippians 3:7-9). When that principle was not at stake, however, he was willing to compromise in order to maintain unity (Romans 14:1-23; 1 Corinthians 8:1-13). As a famous statement on Christian unity puts it, "In essentials, unity; in nonessentials, liberty; in all things, charity."[2]

How ironic, then, that Paul and Barnabas, who had become such friends and colleagues, couldn't agree on a staffing decision and as a result parted company (Acts 15:36-41). Some think Paul was right; making a quitter part of the team was bound to undercut the mission. Others think Barnabas was right, especially since he had accepted and mentored Paul through his anti-Christian past. Instead of debating who was right, perhaps we should see this dispute as an example of God working for good in all things (Romans 8:28). The split launched two mission teams, thus multiplying the spread of the good news.

After circulating that document years ago, I had a behind-the-scenes debate with a fellow leader over our approach to ministry. After a few months it became clear we just couldn't agree, so instead of risking open disunity, I resigned. As difficult as the experience was, we maintained respect and love for each other as brothers in Christ. In fact, we have since corresponded, met and prayed together. I wonder if that was also the experience of Paul and Barnabas after their parting of ways.

Apply: Think of ministry leaders who are experiencing conflict today. Spend some time praying for each one, that they would come to a place of unity, liberty and charity.

❖

DISCUSSION QUESTIONS

After you've completed the five readings in the section "The First Mission Trip," get together with another person or group to talk about the things you've learned. Begin by sharing the insights you've gained from your own reflection on the passages. Then use the following questions to help you continue the conversation.

1. Has God ever called you to take on a mission for him? How did you know for sure? What happened as you pursued the mission? What where the results and what did you learn? (Acts 13:1-12)

2. When have you experienced opposition or resistance to ministry you've been involved in? How did you respond, and what was the result? (Acts 13:1-12)

3. Can you think of a sermon or Christian book that has powerfully affected you? What was the message and how did it change your actions? (Acts 13:13-52)

4. What makes a person fit or unfit for ministry today? When a person fails, how do we know if and when to give them a second chance? (Acts 13:13-52)

5. Describe some successful ministries today. What makes them successful? Do you think the church and Christians have a healthy view of success? (Acts 14:1-28)

6. Think of a time when a ministry experience didn't go as planned. What was the result and what did you learn? In what way is "failure" a good thing? (Acts 14:1-28)

7. In your world, what is the most significant church controversy today? Why is it such a big issue, and what would it take to resolve it? (Acts 15:1-21)

8. Can you think of a contemporary disagreement on Christian principles that had a happy ending? What happened? (Acts 15:1-21)

9. How would you respond to a nonbeliever who said, "The church is so divided today, I don't think I could ever become a Christian"? (Acts 15:22-41)

10. Based on your experiences, what have you learned about resolving personal disagreements with other Christians? (Acts 15:22-41)

[WEEK SEVEN]

More Mission Trips

In our next five readings, we'll ride shotgun with Paul and his companions as they set off on another missionary journey, one that begins in the missional church of Antioch and ends with Paul's Spirit-inspired decision to go to Jerusalem. Along the way we'll see Paul preaching and church planting throughout what today is Turkey, Macedonia and Greece.

What makes this section interesting to us, especially as we reflect on what it takes to make a difference for God today, are several realities of the mission team experience of Paul and his companions. The first reality is that even in the most effective ministry endeavors, we are likely to encounter a mix of openness and opposition. We sometimes assume that if we are serving God, everything will be smooth. After all, "if God is for us, who can be against us?" (Romans 8:31). While it's true that God is with us as we do his will, it doesn't mean our work will be easy. Even though Paul was clearly on a mission from God, in these readings we'll see him imprisoned in Philippi, run out of town in Thessalonica, ridiculed in Athens, rejected in Corinth and caught in a riot in Ephesus. Those aren't the kind of stories we want to include in the newsletter to supporters back home.

And yet, Paul's missionary efforts were extraordinarily fruitful. Not only did he share the good news and plant churches in the Middle East, but he also took the gospel to Macedonia, the gateway to Europe, which led to the spread of the church to the entire world. So the bottom line is that openness and opposition are part of real ministry.

A second reality of Paul's mission team experience is that it included men and women serving God together. Of course, we are most familiar with the men—Silas, Timothy and several others. But the team also included Priscilla, wife of Aquila, who traveled with the team, sailed on the ship with Paul and even risked her life for the gospel. Luke, the historian recording these events, doesn't seem to have a "gender-neutral" or politically correct agenda in mentioning Priscilla. She was just a member of the team.

A third reality is that Paul and his companions were a team, not a family. Well meaning though it may seem, expecting a mission group to be "our family" sets us up for disappointment. Families don't change; teams do, as we'll see in these readings. The fact is, a mission team can never take the place of a true family. But that doesn't mean we won't form close relationships with those we serve alongside. As with the church in Ephesus, sometimes the bonds we form with members of a mission team can be stronger than those of our family.

So get ready to join the team with Paul and see what best practices you can identify for your mission team experiences today.

DAY THIRTY-ONE: Jailhouse Rock

Prepare: What have been some turning points in your life? Spend a few moments reflecting on the ways God has led you at the major crossroads in your journey.

Read: Acts 16:1-40

Reflect: Paul was no paper pusher. With the Council at Jerusalem behind him, Paul was itching to get "out of the office" and back to what he did best: traveling, preaching and planting churches. It's important to recognize what we're good at in ministry; some are builders, others are maintainers, and the church needs both. But there's no question about Paul—he was a builder (Romans 15:20).

That's why Paul got into a predicament in Philippi. He was breaking new turf for the good news in this important Roman city when he attracted both spiritual and economic resistance. The ensuing jailbreak was no less miraculous than Peter's escape (Acts 12:1-19), and reminds us that those who are truly pursuing God's will are never hopeless.

But the punch line of Luke's account is the jailer's question, "Sirs, what must I do to be saved?" (16:30). Some may think the jailer was afraid the prisoners would take revenge, and was begging for mercy, or that he wanted to cut a fast deal, since jailers were executed for allowing their prisoners to escape. What seems clear from the context, however, is that the earthquake had shaken him spiritually, exposing his need for God. That's why Paul immediately saw it as a ministry opportunity, which led to the salvation of an entire family. If we want to make a difference for God today, we too must learn to recognize and appropriately step into the stress and trauma of the people around us.

This passage also demonstrates an important, yet often overlooked, principle about finding God's will. Did you notice that Paul and his companions encountered three red lights—on the edges of Asia, Mysia and Bithynia—before they got a green light to enter Macedonia? That should give us a new perspective on ministry roadblocks.

The significance of God's negative leading here is that he was leaving Paul no option other than to cross the northern Aegean Sea. From the perspective of history we now know that this was a turning point in the growth of the church. It was at this juncture that the gospel spread from the Middle East to Europe; Macedonia is the gateway between the two continents. From Europe the good news spread to the rest of the world, and eventually to you and me. True, it took centuries to play out. But it never would have happened if Paul hadn't understood that God leads us by both saying yes and no.

Apply: What is the biggest roadblock in your life right now? Instead of asking God to remove it, spend some time asking God to show you what he's saying to you through it.

DAY THIRTY-TWO: Flexible Ministry

Prepare: Hum or sing as many verses of "Amazing Grace" as you can remember before beginning your time in God's Word today.

Read: Acts 17:1-34

Reflect: Part of my ministry with Scripture Union has been to speak at churches and Christian conferences in the United States and around the world. I take seriously the need to prepare for these opportunities by creating speaking notes for each message. But over the years I've learned that no matter how well I plan, things often change by the time I arrive, so I must be ready to adapt.

By this time in his mission career, the apostle Paul had mastered the art of ministry flexibility, which is why he was such an effective evangelist and church planter. It's obvious he came to town with a plan: go to the synagogue and make the case for Christ using the Scriptures (17:2-3, 10, 17). It's also obvious that things rarely went according to script, as we see in the three city-wide missions described in our reading today.

In Thessalonica, Paul encountered the usual mix of openness and opposition, a combination he was getting used to. *Oh brother, not another riot!* The variable in the equation this time was the help of Jason, a believer who was willing to put his resources and reputation on the line for the gospel. Even if we aren't called to a frontline role like Paul, we can still be bold and courageous in supporting those who are.

In Berea, the surprise was an eager receptiveness to revisiting the Scriptures. *That's the last thing I expected!* In many Western countries today the influence of the Bible is rapidly evaporating. Even so, I've seen a new interest in God's Word, so long as Christians don't force it on others. The best way to promote the Bible is to be excited about reading and living it ourselves.

But it was in Athens that Paul tried something really new: he stepped out of the synagogue and into the Areopagus, a place where city leaders heard lectures on religion, morals and education.[1] In many ways Athens resembled the postmodern society of today; there were lots of spiritual ideas floating around, but no absolute truth. Let's take a closer look at how Paul presented Christ in such an environment.

The first thing we notice is he was respectful; mocking nonbelievers is not an effective way to gain a hearing. Second, Paul affirmed that his listeners were on a spiritual journey (17:22-23), even though he knew they were headed in the wrong direction. Third, he avoided Christian jargon and tried to communicate using ideas they already accepted, including nature (17:24-25), the universal search for God (17:26-27) and even their own literature (17:28). But finally, after earning the right to be heard, he preached "the good news about Jesus and the resurrection" (17:18, 29-31). Being clear about the gospel, while being able to improvise in how one explains it—that was Paul's approach to helping people understand the good news.

Apply: In a paragraph, write the essence of the good news as you understand it. Now think of a non-Christian friend or acquaintance and rewrite the paragraph in terms that would make sense to them.

DAY THIRTY-THREE: The Mission Team Experience

Prepare: "My soul thirsts for God, for the living God. When can I go and meet with God?" (Psalm 42:2). Ask God to meet you in his Word today.

Read: Acts 18:1-28

Reflect: Have you ever been part of a mission team—that is, a group from your church, school or youth group who spend a few weeks on some kind of outreach project? You travel together, eat together, live together, even raise funds together. But you do it all to accomplish a specific ministry objective, whether in a rural area of a faraway country, or in an inner-city neighborhood near where you live.

Our passage gives us a glimpse into the mission team experience of the apostle Paul, and it's instructive to consider what that was like. The first thing we notice is that the team had a changing cast of characters. It began with Barnabas and Paul, but reorganized into Paul and Silas. Along the way they picked up Timothy, but lost John Mark, then joined up with Aquila and Priscilla, who recruited and trained Apollos. They weren't a family; they were a team, and the players changed. Also, we shouldn't overlook the fact that Paul had a woman on his team; Priscilla was on the boat with her husband and the other men (18:2, 18). She too was a fellow worker who risked her life for the gospel (Romans 16:3-4).

Another reality of Paul's mission team experience hinted at in this passage is fundraising. Of all the tasks required for doing ministry today, that's at the bottom of everyone's list. But notice that Paul viewed resource gathering as part of his role; in Corinth, he took a day job to pay the bills (18:3). In fact, Paul is probably the most proactive fundraiser in the Bible, as we see from the letters he later wrote to the church in Corinth (1 Corinthians 16:1-4; 2 Corinthians 8-9). For Paul and his companions, fundraising wasn't a necessary evil. It was an essential part of ministry.

The thing that stands out most in this passage is the way God intervened to reassure Paul (Acts 18:9-10). I remember a ministry trip I once took. I had traveled all day, was hungry and tired, and found myself sitting alone in a dreary Chick-fil-A restaurant just before closing time. Honestly, I was discouraged, and the best I could do was pray, *Lord, if you aren't in this, then what I'm doing here makes no sense.* The next day I had a breakthrough.

I doubt there was a Chick-fil-A in Corinth, but I'm certain Paul needed encouragement. In addition to the hardships of travel, preaching and fundraising, he had the constant threat of physical abuse and spiritual opposition (18:6). One of the best things about the mission team experience is that it often pushes us to the edge of our ability to cope, and in so doing forces us to rely on God's power more completely.

One more detail stands out: verse 24 begins "Meanwhile . . ." At the same time Paul was experiencing his challenges and breakthroughs, things were happening elsewhere; in this case, Apollos was beginning what became a significant preaching ministry (18:27-28). It reminds us that the mission doesn't depend on me. We all have a part to play, but God is the mission director.

Apply: Make a list of people you know who are serving in some kind of ministry, either full time or as volunteers. Next to each name jot down a way you could offer encouragement. Over the next month, see if you can complete each one.

DAY THIRTY-FOUR: The Real Problem

Prepare: "Be strong and courageous. Do not be terrified; do not be discouraged, for the LORD your God will be with you wherever you go" (Joshua 1:9). How might this verse apply to you today?

Read: Acts 19:1-41

Reflect: By this point, Paul and his companions were getting used to opposition. As we've discovered, it was usually driven by jealousy; the religious leaders didn't like anything that threatened their status in the community. But this passage uncovers the real problem: Luke tells us that some in Ephesus "*refused* to believe" (19:9). Today there are a growing number of authors and speakers making the case for unbelief, and the media seems to delight in promoting them. But no matter how free thinking or insightful it may seem, willfully choosing to turn away from God is always a dangerous move.

But it wasn't just the religious leaders who wanted to thwart the growth of the church. In Ephesus the opposition took two other forms. The first was *commercialism*. Even though the idol makers seemed to understand their products were phony (19:26), they vehemently fought for the right to keep selling them. Throughout history, commercial interests have been the justification for all kinds of evil— for example, slavery. And while it's true that a growing economy is part of a healthy society, any business model out of alignment with God's priorities is a powerful force for evil. Perhaps Paul's experience in Ephesus was part of what motivated him to write, "For the love of money is a root of all kinds of evil" (1 Timothy 6:10).

The second issue was *spiritual opposition*. In a sense, this could describe all the resistance Paul and his companions faced up to this point. But again, in Ephesus the real problem was clearly exposed; many had willingly given themselves over to the forces of evil. Fortunately, "God did extraordinary miracles through Paul" to defeat the evil (19:11), which cleared the way for the good news to be heard and accepted. Spiritual warfare is not just a topic for charismatic churches. Any time we are truly making a difference for God, truly expanding his kingdom, we are bound to meet with some kind of spiritual resistance. "In the name of Jesus" is not just a good way to end a mealtime prayer. For those on the frontlines of ministry, it is the power and protection of God.

In the end, the Ephesians realized there was no reason for their ridiculous riot, so all their opposition fizzled (19:35-41), like a party balloon losing its air. What's most amazing, however, is that in spite of jealousy, commercialism, spiritual warfare and even riots, Paul never stopped pursuing his mission. In fact, the opposition caused him to up his game. It was in Ephesus that he decided to take the fight to the stronghold of his opponents: Jerusalem (19:21). Paul's attitude was,

"Let me at 'em," because he was convinced that "if God is for us, who can be against us?" (Romans 8:31).

Apply: What forms of opposition have you faced in the ministries you've been part of? How did you respond to them?

DAY THIRTY-FIVE: Ministry Snapshots

Prepare: Who are the people you feel closest to in life? And in the church? Spend a few moments praying for these people today.

Read: Acts 20:1-38

Reflect: A few years ago I spent ten days traveling throughout South Korea speaking in churches about Bible reading revival. It was physically challenging and spiritually exhilarating. But the most rewarding part was working with three colleagues from Scripture Union South Korea. We prayed together, ate together, stayed overnight in homes together and shared a lot of "windshield time" traveling together. I discovered that the day-to-day experience of living with those committed to the same ministry made us more effective as a mission team. Our current passage gives us several snapshots from the mission team experience of the apostle Paul.

The first snapshot is of the seven men who traveled with Paul and whose job was to prepare the way for his ministry efforts (20:4-5). From today's vantage point it may seem that Paul was the marquee player in the first-century church. But he couldn't have been as effective without a band of brothers like this. Today, it's easy to focus on the work of a few Christian leaders, and we should be thankful for those who attempt great things for God. But we should not overlook the importance of anonymous mission teams. God does great things through them too. Plus, he uses the mission team experience to refine us in ways few other Christian activities can.

The second snapshot is of Eutychus (20:7-12), the young man who fell from the window and in so doing became the patron saint of sleepy churchgoers ever since. But Paul's belief that God would intervene, and his ability to stay on message after the interruption, show just how focused on ministry he was. That's what makes both individuals and teams effective for God.

The final snapshot is of Paul's farewell moment with the Ephesian Elders (20:13-38). Like a seasoned parent, Paul knew what these church leaders were about to go through (20:29), so he offered two directives to help them survive. First, he said, "Keep watch *over yourselves.*" We shouldn't tell the world to live by God's Word when research shows Bible reading among churchgoers is declining. The best way to bring biblical values to secular society is for the church to rediscover its own Book. Second, Paul said, "Be shepherds" (20:28). The image of a shepherd caring for God's people reverberates throughout Scripture and finds its culmination in Jesus Christ, the Good Shepherd. If we want to know how to strengthen the church today, the quick answer is this: live like Jesus.

Apply: Make a list of three things you could do in the next week to live like Jesus. Now pray for God's help to do so.

DISCUSSION QUESTIONS

After you've completed the five readings in the section "More Mission Trips," get together with another person or group to talk about the things you've learned. Begin by sharing the insights you've gained from your own reflection on the passages. Then use the following questions to help you continue the conversation.

1. Have you ever received a clear call from God? What form did it take, and how did you respond? (Acts 16:1-40)

2. In your own words, how would you respond to a friend or loved one who said to you, "What must I do to be saved?" What does it mean to believe in the Lord Jesus today? (Acts 16:1-40)

3. How would you change your approach in order to share the good news with those who oppose the gospel? Those who are seeking? (Acts 17:1-34)

4. How can we contend for the truth of the gospel today in a society that believes there is no such thing as absolute truth? (Acts 17:1-34)

5. How can you know when it's time to give up on a mission effort? Can you share experiences? (Acts 18:1-28)

6. What's your view of women in ministry? How does the Bible inform or shape that view? What are some principles that should guide men and women serving together on a mission team? (Acts 18:1-28)

7. Have you been involved in some kind of spiritual warfare? What happened and what did you learn from the experience? (Acts 19:1-41)

8. What have been the dangers facing ministries that you've been part of? How can we know when to take risks for God? (Acts 19:1-41)

9. What was the closest mission team experience you've ever had? What made it such a meaningful experience? (Acts 20:1-38)

10. What are some principles for ending a relationship, or at least saying goodbye to someone with whom you've closely worked? (Acts 20:1-38)

Part Four

THE ESSENTIAL QUESTION

[WEEK EIGHT]

Paul's Journey to Jerusalem

The first man to defeat heavyweight boxing champion Mohammed Ali was Joe Frazier. He did it by using a daring strategy: he walked straight up to his opponent, took his best punches and kept coming. In the next five readings we'll see the apostle Paul using the Joe Frazier style of ministry. He walked straight into Jerusalem, home base of his increasingly violent opposition, and confronted them head on.

On one level, Paul's strategy reveals his incredible courage. He wasn't afraid of the religious officials, many of whom he knew personally from his days as a Pharisee. And he also wasn't intimidated by all the nasty things they had done to stop him. Personal courage must be among the qualities of anyone who wants to make a difference for God.

The source of Paul's courage was his rock-solid conviction that he was on a mission for God, and therefore that God would be with him all the way. Luke even tells us that when things looked the most hopeless, "The Lord stood near Paul and said, 'Take courage!'" (Acts 23:11). And as we've already seen in our journey through Acts, this wasn't the first time God had intervened to guide and encourage his servant (Acts 18:9-10).

But perhaps the most notable feature of this section is that here we encounter what I have called "the essential question." When Paul faced his accusers on the steps of a Roman barracks, he defended himself by telling the story of his conversion (Acts 22:3-21). In this account of his Damascus Road experience, he included a detail not found in the two other accounts of the same experience (Acts 9; Acts 26). After being confronted by Jesus himself, Paul reported, he responded by saying, "What shall I do, Lord?" (22:10). That's the essential question. Once you've decided to follow Jesus as Savior and Lord, it's the only question that matters. What does God want me to do? It's the question I have invited you to prayerfully wrestle with in this journey through Acts. In fact, if you haven't already done so, as you read this section it would be a good time to write in the Essential Question Journal on page 137.

There's one final theme to watch out for in this section. Although we now know the end of the story—that Paul had an incredible missionary impact and eventually made it to Rome—Paul didn't know that as he was going through it. In fact, to him the situation in Jerusalem may have seemed hopeless and out of control. But what you'll see is that even so, Paul was willing to take the next step and trust his future to God's sovereignty. As he said earlier, "I consider my life worth nothing to me; my only aim is to finish the race and complete the task the Lord Jesus has given me—the task of testifying to the good news of God's grace" (Acts 20:24). That's a sure strategy for making a difference for God in any age.

DAY THIRTY-SIX: Knowing God's Will

Prepare: "Be joyful always; pray continually; give thanks in all circumstances, for this is God's will for you in Christ Jesus" (1 Thessalonians 5:16-18).

Read: Acts 21:1-26

Reflect: Paul definitely needed a smart phone with GPS. After leaving Miletus, he journeyed down the coast of modern Turkey, crossed the Mediterranean Sea and landed in Tyre. His objective was to reach Jerusalem. Paul could have gone to other cities in the region, where he could have planted more churches. So why did he go to Jerusalem, ground zero of his opposition?

Luke tells us it was a result of two things. First, Paul made a decision to go. It's important that we take time to wait on the Lord when facing an important decision. But holding out for "handwriting on the wall" (see Daniel 5:5-6) can sometimes immobilize us. As we see in this passage, God can use our decisions to move us toward his purposes; God steers a moving ship.

The second and more significant factor driving Paul to Jerusalem was the clear leading of the Holy Spirit. That's what we should desire most when facing a decision. But even when we sense the Spirit's leading we still need prayerful discernment. On the surface it may seem that God was giving mixed signals (21:10-11). But a careful examination shows that both Paul and Agabus got it right. God *was* leading Paul to Jerusalem, and he *was* warning it would be difficult. The point is, neither Paul nor Agabus knew God's full plan—and neither will we. Our responsibility is to faithfully seek God's direction for the next step while trusting the final outcome to him.

Our passage ends with an example of the importance of prayerful dialogue in seeking God's will. James, the leader of the Jewish wing of the church, and Paul, a pioneer of the Gentile wing, met again, with the Jerusalem elders, to confront the most divisive issue of their day: How can Jews and Gentiles be in the same church? What's fascinating is how the two men avoided a blowup and maintained unity.

First, they agreed to meet (21:17-18). When you have an issue with another Christian, even a doctrinal issue, is your first instinct to criticize them to others, or invite them to lunch? Next, they shared mutual respect and accountability. Paul reported what he had been doing (21:19); James praised God for the results (21:20). Are you able to affirm God's work in Christian traditions other than your own? These basic steps created the context for discussing a more delicate issue: what to do about the perception that Paul was encouraging believers to reject Jewish customs (21:21).

Some have criticized Paul for agreeing to James's proposal, claiming Paul compromised his principles. To that, John Stott says, "The solution to which they came was not a compromise, in the sense of sacrificing a doctrinal or moral principle, but a concession in the area of practice."[1] This passage is a case study of what Paul meant when he said, "I have become all things to all people so that by all possible means I might save some" (1 Corinthians 9:22).

Apply: Who are the nonbelievers you'll be with in the next week? What would it mean for you to "become all things to all people"?

DAY THIRTY-SEVEN: Outside the Comfort Zone

Prepare: Are you a risk taker? What's your risk tolerance in financial matters? In physical activities? In serving the Lord?

Read: Acts 21:27-36

Reflect: Have you ever done something for God that you knew would be challenging, even dangerous? I find it difficult to take risks. I'd much rather stay on the safe path for God. Yet in spite of my natural tendency I have to admit I've grown the most, and accomplished the most, when I've stepped, or been pushed, outside my comfort zone.

That's what happened to Paul here; he was way outside the comfort zone. Agabus and other prophets said this day was coming. Even the Holy Spirit warned him. But Paul went to Jerusalem because the Holy Spirit also made clear he should go.

The Jewish leaders whipped the crowd into a violent frenzy. Their shouts for the death penalty had an eerie resemblance to the final days of Jesus (21:36). But why were these religious men so threatened by a defrocked Pharisee with no organization, no militia and no money?

We get a clue in verse 28. The leaders accused Paul of being against "our" law. Not God's law, or even the law of Moses; it was our law, our rules, our system. What's clear from this passage, and from world history ever since, is that when religion becomes a means for human control it is one of the most dangerous things on earth. And that's not the good news.

I wonder if Paul ever second-guessed his decision to go to Jerusalem. It can be physically stressful and spiritually confusing when a step of faith takes us into a sinkhole. But as we'll soon see in Paul's experience, when God is leading, even ministry setbacks can lead to spiritual breakthroughs. That's why, in spite of the growing chaos, Paul could be confident that God was in charge.

Apply: Think of a little risk God may be asking you to take for him in the week ahead. Spend some time praying about it and then, if you feel God's peace about it, commit to action.

DAY THIRTY-EIGHT: The Essential Question

Prepare: Take a few minutes to remember the story of how you first encountered Jesus. Then, thank God for the people and experiences that caused you to say yes to him.

Read: Acts 21:37–22:21

Reflect: If I had just escaped from an angry mob trying to kill me, the last thing I'd do is willingly go back and engage my enemies on the very topic that caused the upset. But that's exactly what Paul did here, and it reminds us how spiritually "strong and courageous" he was (see Deuteronomy 31:6).

How do you communicate the gospel to those who don't want to hear it? That was Paul's challenge as he began speaking to this crowd of angry religious leaders from the steps of the Roman military barracks called the Antonia Fortress. This crowd already knew everything they wanted to know about God. Anything Paul said would only set them off.

As a follower of Christ today, you may have faced similar, though less volatile, situations. The reality is, no matter how you spin it, telling people they need to repent of their sin and accept Jesus Christ can cause friction. Paul handled the situation by simply telling his story, the unvarnished facts of what God had done in his life. That's a good strategy for today, because it's hard to argue with a changed life.

Paul also built his testimony around three questions. The first was, *"Who are you, Lord?"* (22:8). The blinding light and voice from heaven forced him to reevaluate a lifetime of religious assumptions, something he wanted his listeners to do. The second question was, *"What shall I do, Lord?"* (22:10). If Jesus really was alive, then it required a response. The final question came from Paul's first spiritual director, Ananias, *"What are you waiting for?"* (22:16). There's a time to debate spiritual ideas, but there's also a time to make a decision. That was the point of Paul's speech.

This passage brings us to the heart of the journey we've been taking through Acts. If you truly are a follower of Jesus, and if you truly want to make a difference for him with your life, then the question, "What shall I do, Lord?" becomes *your* essential question. What mission, what challenge, what need, what area of Christian service has God brought to your mind and heart as you've progressed through this study?

As we've discovered, God had an assignment for Paul, one that would change his life and the world forever. Yours probably won't be as remarkable as Paul's, and I hope not as stressful! But whatever God calls you to do is no less important, because it's part of his plan and it could change *your* world forever. Maybe the best way to get started is to follow the advice of Oswald Chambers, author of the classic devotional *My Utmost for His Highest*, when he said, "Trust God and do the next thing."[2] How does that help you begin to answer your essential question today?

Apply: Turn to the Essential Question Journal at the back of this book. Pray, and then make a start at answering Paul's question, "What shall I do, Lord?"

DAY THIRTY-NINE: Blessed Assurance

Prepare: "Blessed assurance, Jesus is mine! O what a foretaste of glory divine! Heir of salvation, purchase of God, born of his Spirit, washed in his blood."[3] Reflect on the words of this beloved hymn.

Read: Acts 22:22–23:11

Reflect: *Hee Haw* was a popular television program in the 1970s. A recurring comedy skit had four hillbilly characters sitting on a porch telling sad jokes and singing, "Gloom, despair, agony on me . . . if it weren't for bad luck, I'd have no luck at all." I wonder if the apostle Paul ever felt that way. It's natural to assume that if we've decided to follow Jesus and are serving him, our way will be smooth. But that wasn't Paul's experience, and it probably won't be ours either.

What set these Jewish leaders off again was they just couldn't accept the idea that God's plan of salvation included Gentiles (22:21-22). That may not be an issue for the church today, but are we free of prejudice? People say that in America the most segregated hour of the week is 11:00 to 12:00 on Sunday morning, the time when many people go to church. Changing that picture will require more than just adding a few multiracial photos to the brochure. Change starts by smiling, talking and making friends with people who are different from us. That's important because the grand finale for the church is a great multitude "from every nation, tribe, people and language, standing before the throne and in front of the Lamb" (Revelation 7:9).

Paul understood his struggles had nothing to do with bad luck. As he wrote to his dear friends back in Ephesus, "Our struggle is not against flesh and blood, but against the rulers, against the authorities, against the powers of this dark world and against the spiritual forces of evil in the heavenly realms" (Ephesians 6:12). That was the deeper reality in Paul's heated exchange with the high priest, Ananias, whom history reveals as a corrupt religious leader.[4] Some criticize Paul for his angry sarcasm here, especially since Jesus responded so calmly in a similar situation (John 18:22-23). But there's a time for righteous indignation and this was it. In any case, Paul had the presence of mind to lob a theological hot potato into the discussion, thereby turning the leaders' attacks away from him toward each other.

We're left with the question: How did Paul keep going through all his troubles? The answer comes at the very end of the passage: "The Lord stood near Paul" to renew his courage and affirm his mission (Acts 23:11). Without that, Paul surely would have been overwhelmed. God might not intervene in quite the same way when we face ministry struggles today. It's more likely he'll encourage us through Scripture, prayer, a word from a Christian friend or even a timely experience. The point is, serving God involves struggle, so we must look to him for assurance and guidance every step of the way.

Apply: Prayerfully set the following goal for today: smile at one person different from yourself and make a point of talking to him or her in a friendly way.

DAY FORTY: The Paradox of Ministry

Prepare: "God, grant me the serenity to accept the things I cannot change, the courage to change the things I can, and wisdom to know the difference."[5]

Read: Acts 23:12-35

Reflect: Paul's predicament reads like a good thriller: an assassination plot by a group of extremists, clandestinely supported by corrupt officials; a powerful army coming to the rescue, secretly guided by a vulnerable boy. But this is no novel—Paul faced a real and present danger.

Some Christians think if they are truly following God they shouldn't have to use human strategies to accomplish his purposes. Just let go and let God! But here, even as a prisoner, Paul took initiative to save himself; he schemed with his nephew and a centurion to gain freedom and continue his mission to Rome.

So was it God's plan or human effort that made the difference? The answer is both, and that's the paradox of ministry. If we've taken time to genuinely seek God's will, and we have his peace about it, then action is a way of showing our trust in God. That's what a step of faith is all about.

This passage also reminds us that God sometimes uses secular officials to accomplish his purposes. Claudius Lysias, the Roman commander of Antonia Fortress, was not a member of "the Way," but at least he was trying to do the right thing, and that enabled God's plan to move forward. It's true, there are times when Christians are called to resist the evils of government, but that shouldn't be our default position. Perhaps it was Paul's experience with Claudius Lysias that later prompted him to write, "For the one in authority is God's servant for your good" (Romans 13:4 NIV 2011). Christians must respect government officials because their authority comes from God and he uses them to do his will (Romans 13:1-7).

That's not to say old Claudius was a super saint. His letter, while basically truthful, rearranged the facts in a way that made him look good—typical bureaucratic behavior. What's harder to fathom is why he felt Paul needed such massive secret service protection: four hundred soldiers and seventy horsemen for one measly Roman citizen! Claudius thought he was just bumping Paul's case upstairs. But now we see God was using this series of bureaucratic decisions to bring the good news of Jesus Christ to the most powerful city in the world.

Buried in this passage is a significant detail: Paul had a sister (23:16). It's intriguing that Paul's family system was one more variable God used to accomplish his plan. No sister, no nephew, no way to alert the commander, no more mission to Rome. The episode came to a positive end for Paul, but we are left to wonder if the plotters kept their word (Acts 23:14).

Apply: What kind of relationship do you have with your family? Think of some practical thing you could do today to forward God's purposes for a member of your family.

DISCUSSION QUESTIONS

After you've completed the five readings in the section "Paul's Journey to Jerusalem," get together with another person or group to talk about the things you've learned. Begin by sharing the insights you've gained from your own reflection on the passages. Then use the following questions to help you continue the conversation.

1. Have you ever made a decision that others questioned but that you felt was what God wanted you to do? What happened? (Acts 21:1-26)

2. What is the most controversial issue facing your church or denomination today? Is there something in Paul's experience that applies? (Acts 21:1-26)

3. In what ways, if any, has religious tradition become more important in your church than following Jesus? What's the good of religious tradition? (Acts 21:27-36)

4. Have you, or anyone you know, been arrested for protesting or demonstrating based on your faith? When do you think such action is justified? (Acts 21:27-36)

5. Share the story of how you first encountered Jesus, and how your eyes were opened to who he really is. (Acts 21:37–22:21)

6. Share your thoughts on an answer to your own essential question, "What shall I do, Lord?" (Acts 21:37–22:21)

7. What expressions of irrational hate are you aware of? What's the cause and what can you do as a Christian to promote peace in these situations? (Acts 22:22–23:11)

8. In what ways, if any, do you think prejudice has affected the Christian church? How could you or your church better express God's love to a needy world? (Acts 22:22–23:11)

9. What's your view of the government in your country? How does, or should, your faith influence this view? (Acts 23:12-35)

10. Have you ever had an experience that seemed out of control at the time but in retrospect you realized God had a specific plan? What happened? (Acts 23:12-35)

[WEEK NINE]

Paul's Roman Trial

Felix, Festus and Agrippa—those are the Roman officials we'll meet in this next set of readings. As you'll see, all three have lots of worldly power, and all three take their turn presiding over a trial of the powerless apostle Paul. What's amazing is that in each case Paul comes away with the win, and in so doing advances God's plan to spread the good news throughout the civilized world.

Felix had mixed motives. On the one hand he was familiar with "the Way"—that is, the emerging first-century church—and he seemed to be looking for an approach that would fairly resolve Paul's case. But on the other hand Felix dragged the trial out for two long years, hoping for a bribe, and in the end tried to use Paul for his own political gain.

Festus inherited Paul's case and brought a new perspective to the proceedings: he was partial to the religious leaders who were out to kill the "apostle to the Gentiles" (Romans 11:13). That motivated Paul, himself a Roman citizen, to make a dramatic legal maneuver: "I appeal to Caesar!" he shouted. Paul appealed to the Supreme Court of his day, and it guaranteed him a free ticket to Rome, the very place God wanted him to go.

Along the way, one last Roman authority tried his hand at Paul's case. But as the courtroom dialogue unfolded, it became clear that even the powerful King Agrippa was no match for an evangelist like Paul. "Do you think that in such a short time you can persuade me to be a Christian?" said Agrippa. "Short time or long," Paul replied, "I pray to God that not only you but all who are listening to me today may become what I am, except for these chains" (Acts 26:28-29). That's evangelistic chutzpah!

As you make your way through the Roman trial of Paul, keep an eye out for two themes. First, notice the *power of focus*. In many ways, Paul lost control of his ministry. He was caught in the Roman justice system and vulnerable to the whims of those in charge. But because Paul stayed focused on his calling, "testifying to the gospel of God's grace" (Acts 20:24), he had an effective ministry anyway.

The second theme is the *power of God*. Beneath the turbulent surface waters of these trials, the strong current of God's plan was at work, using the seemingly negative situation to get his servant and his message from Jerusalem to Rome. As you're about to see, these next five readings are strong encouragement for anyone serving God in the face of opposition today.

DAY FORTY-ONE: The Inconvenient Truth

Prepare: Begin your time of worship with the ACTS prayer method: Adoration, Confession, Thanksgiving, Supplication.

Read: Acts 24:1-27

Reflect: Tertullus is one of the biggest phonies in the Bible; he gives lawyers a bad name. First, he complimented Felix on achieving "peace" and "reforms," but everyone present knew what history now tells us: Felix was a brutal Roman official, despised by the Jews.[1] Next, Tertullus professed "profound gratitude" for Felix's tremendous leadership, a claim that would have caused even the Romans to roll their eyes. Finally, he accused Paul of being a religious "troublemaker," a charge hardly worth all the fuss (Acts 24:2-5).

Tertullus's charade raises an important question for those in frontline ministry today: How should we respond to untrue criticism and unfair treatment from those who oppose the gospel? What's interesting is that Paul's main concern was not the injustice being done to him. Rather, his concern was to continue sharing the good news, and we should note how he accomplished that.

First, he *responded* to the charges (24:10-13). Tertullus accused Paul of stirring up riots when in fact it was the religious leaders who had instigated them. Paul simply stated for the record that he went to the temple to pray, and he invited Felix to check the facts with eyewitnesses. Knowing that both our actions and motives are pure gives us great freedom and power in responding to our critics.

Second, Paul *redirected* the discussion to spiritual matters by saying the real issue was not riots, but the resurrection. Even though Paul had a lot in common with his accusers (24:14-16), the elephant in the room was his claim that Jesus rose from the dead. That's still the foundation of the Christian faith. Finally, Paul *recounted* part of his spiritual journey (24:17-18). Simply telling people how God has worked in our lives is an effective way to witness for Christ.

Apparently Paul was getting through to Felix, but he wasn't ready to commit (24:22-26). Maybe he thought joining the Way would cause him to lose reputation or power. The text says he was hoping for a bribe. But Felix's excuse was perhaps more honest than he intended— becoming a follower of Jesus just wasn't "convenient" (24:25). That's still the case for many people today. Sometimes the objection that is most difficult to overcome is not from bad people opposing the gospel; rather it's from good people who don't want to be inconvenienced by the truth.

Apply: What untrue criticism or unfair treatment have you received for doing ministry? How does this passage help you respond to such situations?

DAY FORTY-TWO: "I Appeal to Caesar!"

Prepare: How would you describe your life today—focused, hectic, busy, discouraging? Spend a few moments asking for God's peace and presence, regardless of what you are experiencing.

Read: Acts 25:1-12

Reflect: Several years ago I was pulled over for a traffic violation by a policeman in Philadelphia. He said I ran a red light. I claimed the light was yellow. We argued for a while but he had the badge and that gave him power over me. When the officer handed me the ticket he said, "If you want, you can appeal this in traffic court." Sure of my innocence, I decided to take my case downtown. That's what happens in this passage. After arguing over his alleged violation, Paul famously took his case downtown: "I appeal to Caesar!" (Acts 25:8-11).

In this passage, we also sense a change in Paul's tone. So far in our journey through Acts we've seen him harassed, opposed, manhandled, beaten and even stoned. But no matter what, Paul stayed focused on sharing the good news with Jew and Gentile alike. Here, after two years of house detention while the religious leaders plotted to do him in, he seems to be saying, *"That's it! I demand my rights!"*

That raises two intriguing questions for those who want to make a difference for God today. First, when is it right to fight back against opposition? After all, didn't Jesus say, "turn to them the other cheek" (Matthew 5:39 NLT)? But what if you have tried that and it hasn't worked? It's true that our first instinct must always be to pray and trust God; the Bible contains many accounts of divine intervention to solve impossible problems (for example, Exodus 14:13-14). But sometimes, as we see in this passage, it's right to stick up for ourselves. God can use that to produce a ministry breakthrough too.

The second question underlying this passage is a variation of the first: When is it right to help God accomplish his plan? After all, Paul already knew he was going to testify in both Jerusalem and Rome (Acts 23:11). It's a tough question, one for which there is no cookie-cutter answer. In this case we note that Paul was certain of God's call and willing to completely submit to God's outcome (Acts 25:11). That freed him to take bold action to achieve God's purposes.

When I arrived in traffic court years ago, I sat in the gallery watching the other appeals. Finally it was my turn and I nervously explained my side of the story. The judge looked at me, paused, then dismissed the case. I don't think he believed me, but he had no choice because the accusing officer hadn't shown up. Soon we'll find out the result of Paul's appeal to Caesar. For now, we can only admire the way God was using Paul's faith in action to spread the good news.

Apply: Are you feeling stuck or trapped in some area of your life? Ask God to show you his purpose for the situation, and what action he wants you to take.

DAY FORTY-THREE: Who Is Jesus?

Prepare: This well-known question is still worth considering: If you were put on trial for being a Christian, would there be enough evidence to convict you?

Read: Acts 25:13-27

Reflect: Festus knew how to deal with most of the cases that came his way. If someone committed a crime, throw him in prison. If someone rebelled against the state, crucify him. If a guard messed up, flog him or worse. It was all very black and white—and brutal.

But how should the governor respond to someone like Paul who passionately believed a dead man was alive (Acts 25:19)? That was the underlying problem that had so mystified Festus and his colleague, Agrippa: Who is Jesus? And to complicate matters, they knew Paul was innocent of any crimes (25:25), yet somehow they had to explain it all in a letter to their boss, His Majesty, Caesar himself. As Festus commented, "I was at a loss how to investigate such matters" (25:20).

In a certain way, that's exactly the dilemma twenty-first-century men and women have. We understand money, sex and power. And we know how to research everything else on Wikipedia. But we're at a loss how to find the truth about Jesus Christ.

One obstacle to honest investigation comes from within the church. When Christians seem more interested in marginal issues—like reading only a certain translation of the Bible, or refraining from dancing and movies, or requiring women to dress a certain way—then they are missing the point of the gospel and preventing others from entering the kingdom.

Another obstacle more prevalent outside the church is the modern assumption that there is no such thing as absolute truth. Today, many believe all religions are equally true. So the claim that Christianity is the one true religion seems narrow at best and offensive at worst. But that characterization also misses an important point. Even the Christian religion—that is, its buildings, traditions and hierarchy—isn't the exclusive way to God. Jesus Christ is (John 14:6). That's an important distinction.

In the 1990s, Lee Strobel, an atheist legal editor for the *Chicago Tribune*, took on the challenge of investigating the claims of Christ. He interviewed dozens of experts to determine whether there was sufficient evidence to prove Jesus was the Son of God. Like a good journalist, he asked tough, even skeptical questions. At the conclusion of his quest Strobel wrote a book summarizing his results. *The Case for Christ* is one of the most persuasive explanations of the good news in modern times.

In the end, the key question for Festus and Agrippa, as well as for those inside and outside the church today, is the one Jesus himself asked: "Who do you say I am?" (Matthew 16:15).

Apply: On day fifteen, you made a "case for Christ" for sharing with others. Look at it again and see if you can refine or strengthen your case, based on what you've learned in Acts. Then pray for a new opportunity to share it.

DAY FORTY-FOUR: Paul's *Apologia*

Prepare: What is the spiritual state of the people you'll be with this week or month? Pray that they will become fully committed followers of Jesus.

Read: Acts 26:1-18

Reflect: Years ago I went to a Sunday night evangelism class at our church in West Philadelphia. At the beginning of the course, the pastor gave an assignment of writing a personal mission statement that we would have to read aloud by the end. "I know my testimony," I thought, "so I don't need to write anything down." When the day came to read our statements, the pastor called on me first. When he realized I hadn't done the assignment, to my embarrassment, he moved on to someone else.

In this passage, Paul finally got his chance to stand and deliver his *apologia* (Latin for "the defense of one's beliefs, positions or actions"), and he was ready. In spite of the contrast between his humble position as a prisoner and the "great pomp" of the official Roman setting (Acts 25:23), Paul was not intimidated in the least. Perhaps at times you've been given the opportunity to publicly explain your beliefs about Jesus. It can be challenging, even for longtime believers. That's why it will help us to examine what made Paul so effective in this high-pressure situation.

The first thing we notice is that Paul *knew his audience* (26:1-8). He was aware, for example, of Agrippa's spiritual interests (26:3). In spite of all he'd been through, Paul still cared about the spiritual state of his Roman oppressor. That's because Paul was convinced the good news was not just for "good people." As he later wrote to Timothy, "Christ Jesus came into the world to save sinners—of whom I am the worst" (1 Timothy 1:15). That's the ethos of evangelism.

Paul also had a personal knowledge of his Jewish opponents (26:5). Again, given their repeated attempts to discredit and harm him, Paul might be excused for expressing anger. No doubt they did make him angry at times. But underneath Paul had a brokenhearted love for his countrymen who wouldn't accept Jesus as their Messiah (see Romans 10:1). That's the heartbeat of evangelism.

The second key to Paul's apologia was that he *knew his story* (26:9-18). This is the third time in Acts that we've read of Paul's conversion, and each time the message is basically the same (Acts 9; 22; 26). Even if it lacks the drama of Paul's story, can you quickly retell the basic facts about how you began a relationship with Christ? In this version, Paul emphasized the commissioning God gave him on the Damascus Road; he was to be a "servant" and a "witness" (26:16). Those are still good marching orders for anyone wanting to make a difference for God today.

After the awkward end of my evangelism course years ago, I finally finished the assignment our pastor gave me. Now I keep my personal mission statement, including my testimony and my defense of the gospel, on my laptop so I'm always ready to stand and deliver.

Apply: At the back of this book is a section called "My *Apologia*." Take some time this week to write in it the basics of your testimony and your defense of the gospel.

DAY FORTY-FIVE: The Focused Life

Prepare: When are you most focused in your life? At work? Playing a favorite sport? Working at your job? Serving at church? What accounts for this heightened sense of focus?

Read: Acts 26:19-32

Reflect: What we have in this passage is the second half of Paul's apologia (his defense of the gospel) before King Agrippa, Festus and the Roman court. By now this speech may have a familiar ring since Paul has been defending himself and his message throughout three missionary journeys. But this happens to be the longest and most complete statement Luke has included in Acts, and it has two distinctive elements.

The first is Paul's summary of his own message—repent, turn to God, live right (26:20). That could be the sermon notes of John the Baptist, John Wesley, D. L. Moody, Billy Graham or any great evangelist. But what ignited Paul's evangelistic fervor was his experience on the Damascus Road. As he said, "I was not disobedient to the vision" (26:19). Paul never forgot that life-changing event. Of all the things we've read in our journey through Acts, perhaps the three biggest change-drivers have been the outpouring of the Holy Spirit, Peter's meeting with Cornelius and the conversion of Paul.

The second distinctive element is Paul's claim that his message was not new. In fact, it was firmly rooted in the Old Testament (26:22-23). That's because the big story of the Bible is God's plan of salvation that began in the Garden of Eden and culminated in the birth, death, resurrection and eventual return of his Son, Jesus Christ (Luke 24:44-46). That storyline is what explains the Bible, and all of life.

Throughout Paul's monologue, Festus was sitting on the sidelines—quiet as a time bomb. When he finally blew up (Acts 26:24), it led to one of the most dramatic verbal jousting matches in the Bible. Paul went toe-to-toe with Festus, Agrippa and the entire Roman court (26:25-29). It was an amazing display of Spirit-inspired confidence.

The dialogue gives us an insight into the incredible strength of

Paul's inner game. No matter where he was, no matter what happened to him, Paul stayed focused on his calling (see Romans 1:1-6). That's the lens through which he viewed everything in life.

Paul is a remarkable example of the power of the focused life. And what exactly is it? *To be clear* about your God-given mission, great or small, *to be wholehearted* about pursuing it with everything you have, and then *to be willing* to trust the outcome of your efforts and your entire life to God. That's the way to change your world forever.

Apply: How would you articulate your calling? What would it take for you to live the focused life? Record your thoughts in the Essential Question Journal.

DISCUSSION QUESTIONS

After you've completed the five readings in the section "Paul's Roman Trial," get together with another person or group to talk about the things you've learned. Begin by sharing the insights you've gained from your own reflection on the passages. Then use the following questions to help you continue the conversation.

1. Can you think of a time when someone like Tertullus opposed your efforts to do ministry? What happened and what did you learn from the experience? (Acts 24:1-27)

2. When has God used a delay or setback to forward his purposes in your life? (Acts 24:1-27)

3. What is the most dangerous ministry situation you've ever encountered? What gave you the strength to go through it? (Acts 25:1-12)

4. Paul appealed to Caesar and it forwarded God's plan. How do you know when to take initiative yourself to accomplish God's purposes? (Acts 25:1-12)

5. Why do you think it's so difficult for people today to understand

their need for a Savior? (Acts 25:13-27)

6. Which do you think is a bigger hindrance to the cause of Christ today: the legalism of some inside the church, or the belief that there's no such thing as absolute truth outside the church? Why? (Acts 25:13-27)

7. Discuss what you think are the key points in an apologia for the gospel today. See if you can make an outline of a strong defense of the Christian faith. (Acts 26:1-18)

8. What are the three or four critical moments in your journey of faith so far? (Acts 26:1-18)

9. Share a time when God enabled you to boldly witness for your faith in Jesus. What did you learn and what were the results? (Acts 26:19-32)

10. Share some examples of people today who seem especially effective at communicating Christian truth in a secular environment. What do you learn from these examples? (Acts 26:19-32)

[WEEK TEN]

Paul's Journey to Rome

In our next set of readings we leave the pressures of the courtroom for the thrill of the high seas. Although Luke is a historian, he has a novelist's flare for a dramatic ending, and the final two chapters in Acts capture one of the most exciting stories in the Bible.

As you'll remember, Paul had been stuck in a series of trials before three Roman officials—Felix, Festus and Agrippa. When it became clear he'd never get a fair hearing, and worse, that his enemies were about to do him in, Paul shouted, "I appeal to Caesar!" It was a savvy move because it immediately removed Paul from danger and gave him an all-expenses-paid trip to Rome, the very place God wanted him to preach the gospel.

But getting there proved a challenge. We'll read what amounts to Luke's mission journal of the harrowing trip across the Mediterranean Sea and up the coast of Italy. One thing you'll notice is the rich level of detail in Luke's account—the specifics of the itinerary, the patterns of the wind, even the small details of the ships. These are the observations of an eyewitness and they serve to reinforce the credibility of this biblical account.

The big theme to watch out for in this section is how God accomplished his salvation purpose. In the very first chapter of Acts, after his resurrection but before his ascension, Jesus shared God's plan with his bewildered followers: "You will be my witnesses in Jerusalem, and in all Judea and Samaria, and to the ends of the earth" (Acts 1:8). Really? No doubt that seemed impossible to that first little church of 120 people, and in their own strength, it was. So to accomplish a big audacious goal like that, they'd need the Holy Spirit's help, not just on the Day of Pentecost, but every step of the way. And that's exactly what happened.

By the end of the book of Acts, the church was well on the way to fulfilling God's plan of salvation. The good news had been preached all over the Middle East and had broken into Europe, and churches were springing up everywhere. In the final chapter of Acts, Paul even had an unhindered opportunity to preach the gospel for "two whole years" in the most influential city in the world (Acts 28:30-31). From that beginning, the church has spread across the globe.

There's one last thing I want to say before we come to the end of Acts: thanks for taking this journey with me. Along the way I hope you've gotten a clearer picture of how God wants to use you to make a difference for him. I also hope that the experience of reading through the book of Acts will propel you into a lifetime pattern of meeting God every day in the Bible and prayer.[1] May God richly bless you as you continue meeting him in his Word and serving him in the world.

DAY FORTY-SIX: Mission Journal

Prepare: What is the longest trip you've ever taken? Spend a minute remembering what happened and how you felt about that experience.

Read: Acts 27:1-12

Reflect: For most of my adult life I've kept a journal. For years I used spiral-bound notebooks, but more recently I've switched to an iPad for recording my thoughts. I've discovered that one of the best times for journaling is when I'm traveling, especially for ministry purposes. There's something about being on the road with God that helps me reflect on what he's called me to do.

Our current passage reads like the beginning of Luke's mission journal for the trip to Rome (the word *we* in verse 1 reminds us Luke was an eyewitness). He inventories the odd little group that boarded the ship: Julius the centurion, Luke the journalist, Paul the apostle and a few other prisoners. Like the crew of the *SS Minnow* on the TV show *Gilligan's Island*, the passengers had no idea what was in store for them on their "tour."

That's the way it is with serving God. We set out in a direction, with a certain group of people, but we must be ready for God to change everything along the way. As God said through his prophet Isaiah, "For my thoughts are not your thoughts, neither are your ways my ways" (Isaiah 55:8). As we discovered earlier in Acts, God always has a plan, though we may not always be able to perceive it in real time.

I wonder what Paul was thinking as he sat on the deck staring out at the open sea. Did his thoughts drift back to his early life as a top-gun Pharisee, or to his dramatic encounter with Jesus on the Damascus Road, or to all he'd been through as an "apostle to the Gentiles"? Today we know the result of Paul's ministry: the good news spread "in Jerusalem, and in all Judea and Samaria, and to the ends of the earth" (Acts 1:8). But at the time, Paul had no idea that would happen. That's why it's important to look back, to remember what God has done in the past. It helps us recognize the pattern of what he's doing in the present and encourages us to trust him for the future.

By the end of this short journal entry, as the wind stiffened and the sky darkened, we have a sense that the worst was yet to come. In the face of the impending disaster, Luke notes, Paul stepped up as the spiritual leader (27:9-10), and as we'll see, it would significantly affect the outcome of the trip. That's one thing mission trips, especially difficult ones, can do: create opportunities for shaping spiritual leaders, which the church desperately needs more of today.

Apply: If you've ever kept a journal, take some time to read portions of it today and reflect on what God has been doing in your life. If you don't keep one, start a mini-journal: write down the three biggest things God has done in your life over the past year.

DAY FORTY-SEVEN: A Titanic Ministry

Prepare: What is the greatest area of pressure in your life right now? How are you responding to this situation?

Read: Acts 27:13-26

Reflect: In this passage, Paul's Mediterranean cruise turns into *The Poseidon Adventure*. Before it's all over the voyage will seem more like the *Titanic*. The very thing Paul predicted (27:10) now begins to happen. Perhaps some of the crew members nervously recalled that old saying, "Things always seem the darkest before they go totally black."

How do you respond when things seem the darkest, especially when you are trying to serve God? Some people get mad: *Why is God doing this to me?* But as we've seen throughout the book of Acts, serving God takes us straight into spiritual battle, so it's rarely easy. Remember how all this started? The church in Antioch was committed to intense prayer, fasting and worship before they sent out the mission team (Acts 13:1-3). We need to take spiritual preparation seriously if we expect to weather the inevitable storms of ministry.

As the situation on board spiraled from bad to worse, Luke says, "We finally gave up all hope of being saved" (27:20). Sometimes God takes us to the end of our ability to cope so we can more clearly see his power at work. In fact, for some people, disaster in their health, finances, career or some other area can be the climax that redirects them to Christ. That's an important truth to remember when talking to anyone going through a tough time. But perhaps the greatest value of desperation is that it makes us ready to listen to God in a way that few other things can. Has that ever happened to you?

I love the detail Luke noticed in the midst of the growing crisis: Paul "stood up" (27:21). Like Peter at earlier moments of uncertainty (Acts 1:15; 2:14), there's a time to stand and boldly articulate a spiritual perspective on the situations we're in—that is, to refocus the attention of the group "not on what is seen, but on what is unseen" (2 Corinthians 4:18). But when we do, it's important that our motivation is not to show off or gain personal attention. The last thing anyone needs in the midst of crisis is someone on a spiritual ego trip.

In Paul's case, his confidence was based on his continuing encounter with God (27:23-24). As we've seen, what began on the Damascus Road had become a pattern in his life. God may not intervene in quite the same way for you. But we can all cultivate the habit of meeting God every day in the Bible and prayer, as you've been doing in this study. Over the years I've discovered that prayerfully reading God's Word for the purpose of getting closer to him, not just to get more Bible information, is the best way to experience God and prepare for ministry.

Apply: Think again of the area of greatest pressure in your life at this time. Jot down what you think God is saying and doing in the situation. What unseen purpose do you think is at work?

DAY FORTY-EIGHT: The Shipwreck Moment

Prepare: Have you ever been on a boat or ship that encountered rough waters or even a storm? What was it like, and how did you feel?

Read: Acts 27:27-44

Reflect: There comes a point in any ministry effort when it feels like things have crashed. I call it "the shipwreck moment." Sometimes it's the result of bad planning, sometimes you get overwhelmed by uncontrollable variables, sometimes you meet with spiritual opposition, and sometimes internal discord swamps your efforts. But the reality is, when you serve God, shipwrecks happen.

I remember being part of a team that organized an evangelistic event in a maximum security prison. We wanted to present the gospel to the entire prison population, not just the chapel regulars. So we lined up Stevie Wonder to give a concert, followed by the late Chuck Colson to preach the gospel. It seemed like a great plan until I found myself in the prison gymnasium surrounded by five hundred rowdy maximum security inmates and only a few guards by the doors. Stevie Wonder's music emboldened the inmates to a near riot and our team was lucky to get out unhurt.

In contrast, Paul's shipwreck moment led to two very positive outcomes. The first was the survival of all 276 passengers. Already on this trip we've seen Paul's spiritual leadership. Here he continued by commanding the sailors not to abandon ship, and by encouraging them to gain strength by eating; he even set the example by calmly, prayerfully beginning the meal himself (27:31-35). But notice that Paul's spiritual leadership was not an excuse for mutiny; he was respectful of the centurion, allowing him to make the final decision (27:31). Those in ministry must be careful not to let spiritual jargon mask a power-play motive. Paul didn't need to force his will on Julius because he knew God was at work in the chaos (27:23-24).

The second positive outcome was the increasing faith of those on board. For sure they were desperate, and they were probably beginning to recognize Paul's natural leadership ability. But some also seemed to take a tentative step of faith; the soldiers trusted Paul's prophetic word and jettisoned the lifeboats (27:32). When you reach the point of no return you're ready to take a step of faith.

In spite of the dicey situation in that prison gym years ago, I still remember Chuck Colson preaching about the two thieves on the cross. Given his own history as a Watergate felon, it was a message Chuck could deliver with great conviction. Maybe the event didn't go as we planned, but even so, I'm still thankful that every inmate in that maximum security prison did hear the gospel. The good thing about the shipwreck moment is that it opens the way for God to accomplish his purposes, his way.

Apply: What have you learned from the shipwreck moments in your life? Are you facing such a moment now? What lessons from your past, or from this passage, can you apply to your present situation?

DAY FORTY-NINE: Ministry Along the Way

Prepare: Think of the people who have been the most kind and hospitable to you in your life. Take a few minutes to thank God for their ministry to you. Then pray that God will bless them.

Read: Acts 28:1-10

Reflect: When I was in high school our family took a car trip from Maryland to Massachusetts to be with relatives one Thanksgiving. During the drive an early snowstorm moved in and we had to spend an unplanned night in Connecticut. While we were stranded in a roadside motel, my father took lots of Super 8 movies of me and my siblings frolicking in the snow. Today, whenever we watch those home movies we're all reminded of the wonderful time we had along the way.

In a sense this passage is like Luke's home movies of an unplanned stay for Paul and his companions on the island of Malta. As it turned out, it was a positive experience because the islanders showed them "unusual kindness" (28:2). Publius set the tone for those under his authority with his instinct for hospitality. Is that what outsiders experience when they walk into your church—unusual kindness and hospitality? If we want to make a difference for God today perhaps that's where we need to begin.

But the most striking thing about the stay on Malta is how Paul had opportunities for ministry along the way. Of course his main objective was Rome, the most important city in the world, where he was planning to boldly witness for Christ. With that on his mind, Paul could have said, "I've just been through a stressful few days and I need my rest if I'm going to preach in Rome. I don't have time for random ministry now." But he didn't react that way. Paul took time to heal the father of Publius (28:8), which led to a wider healing ministry on the island.

We must never forget that ministry along the way is just as important as accomplishing a grand mission objective. In fact, when we think about the life of Jesus, most of what he did was ministry along the way. His main objective was to die on the cross for the sins of the world. But along the way he reached out to thousands of random, hurting people. That's what the gospel accounts are all about.

Let's not miss the role of prayer in Paul's ministry. We know from other parts of Acts that God had given Paul a special ability to heal others (19:11-12). Even so, he took time in this instance to pray first. Perhaps he needed insight into the ailing man's real condition. Or maybe Paul wanted to get a sense of God's intention for Publius's father. Either way, prayer was the essential first step. This reminds us that the purpose of prayer in ministry is not just to ask God to act, although that's part of it. It's also to make sure we are in alignment with God's agenda before we attempt great things for him.

One last detail from Luke's home movie is worth replaying: Paul himself received a dramatic healing (28:3-6). It's a reminder that when we are faithfully serving God, in both our big plans and our unplanned ministry along the way, we can trust him to take care of us.

Apply: Jot down a few opportunities for ministry along the way that you are likely to have in the next week or so. Ask God to help you recognize them and be his servant in these situations.

DAY FIFTY: An Everyday Challenge

Prepare: Consider 2 Corinthians 5:20: "We are therefore Christ's ambassadors, as though God were making his appeal through us."

Read: Acts 28:11-31

Reflect: "And so we came to Rome" (28:14). Those six words summarize more than just the conclusion of Luke's mission journal. In a certain way they sum up Paul's entire life. As we've seen in our journey through Acts, Paul grew up as a religious zealot, became a Christian-hating bounty hunter, but then, as a result of his encounter with Jesus Christ, spent the rest of his life preaching the gospel and planting churches. *That's* how he got to Rome.

The question we must ask as we look back on Paul's life is this: Was he a success? From one perspective we could say no. He never stayed put long enough to build an organization, he was always in trouble and finally he was executed.[2] Those aren't the kind of achievements you trumpet in your annual report. But the book of Acts challenges us to take a deeper view of success, both for Paul and for anyone who wants to serve God today.

The question we've been pondering throughout this study, what I've called the *essential question*, is the one Paul himself asked after he met Jesus on the Damascus Road: "What shall I do, Lord?" (Acts 22:10). Once we've decided to follow Jesus, answering that question must become the primary focus of our lives. God gave Paul his answer right away: "This man is my chosen instrument to proclaim my name to the Gentiles and their kings and to the people of Israel" (Acts 9:15 NIV 2011). And now, in the final verse of Acts, we find Paul still at it: "Boldly and without hindrance he preached the kingdom of God and taught about the Lord Jesus Christ" (28:31). Knowing and faithfully pursuing our God-given mission—that's the real definition of success, and by that measure Paul achieved it in the most incredible way.

Now that we've come to the end of our journey together, let's take a moment to remember some of the people we've met along the way.

- *Peter*, the first one to "get it" and "announce it," that God's good news was for everyone

- *Stephen*, the first one to "die for it," and in so doing to become a model for martyrs ever since

- *Philip*, miraculously used to "spread it" to Africa, a place that today has become one of the strongest Christian areas of the world

- *Paul*, the one God used to "expand it," establishing the church among Jews, Gentiles and eventually the whole world

But there's one more person who's been on the journey through Acts, and that's you. You've seen how God used the individuals and small groups of the first-century church to make a difference for him. Now it's your turn. But it's important to realize that answering the essential question is not a one-time event. It's an everyday challenge. "What shall I do, Lord?" is the question that will keep you focused on your God-given mission, whether great or small, for the rest of your life. And that's the way to change your world forever.

Apply: Take some extra time today to record your main insights from this journey through Acts in the Essential Question Journal at the back of this book.

DISCUSSION QUESTIONS

After you've completed the five readings in the section "Paul's Journey to Rome," get together with another person or group to talk about the things you've learned. Begin by sharing the insights you've gained from your own reflection on the passages. Then use the following questions to help you continue the conversation.

1. Have you ever taken a mission trip? Share with each other the things you've learned from your mission experiences. (Acts 27:1-12)

2. Have you ever turned back from a ministry effort because it seemed unwise to proceed? What happened? Does God ever lead us into danger? (Acts 27:1-12)

3. What's the most stressful ministry situation you've ever been in? How did it turn out and what did you learn? (Acts 27:13-26)

4. In what ways does God encourage you when you attempt to do ministry for him? Can you share specific experiences? (Acts 27:13-26)

5. Have you ever experienced a "shipwreck moment," a time when your ministry plan crashed? What happened and what did you learn? (Acts 27:27-44)

6. Romans 8:28 says, "In all things God works for the good of those who love him." Why is that such an encouragement? Can it also be an excuse? (Acts 27:27-44)

7. What are some examples of unusual kindness and hospitality you've seen or experienced? How did it forward the cause of Christ? (Acts 28:1-10)

8. What do you believe about prayer and healing? Can you share some experiences where God used prayer to heal you or someone you know? (Acts 28:1-10)

9. What do you think are the most effective ways to convince people about the truth of the gospel today? Can you share experiences? (Acts 28:11-31)

10. What have been the main themes that stood out to you from your journey through the book of Acts? (Acts 28:11-31)

THE ESSENTIAL QUESTION
JOURNAL

As you take this journey through the book of Acts, use this journal to jot down your insights from the Bible, or your responses to the essential question: "What should I do, Lord?" (Acts 22:10). At the end, you'll have a record of what God has been saying to you.

Insights from my journey through the book of Acts:

Responses to the essential question, "What should I do, Lord?":

MY *APOLOGIA*

Apologia is a Latin word meaning "a defense, especially of one's opinions, position or actions." As you go through the book of Acts, use this space to make notes on your *apologia* for the Christian faith.

- How did you become a follower of Jesus? What's your story of coming to faith?

- What do you believe about Jesus Christ? Who do you say he was?

- How would you articulate the case for Christ in today's world?

- What is your defense for the gospel?

NOTES

Introduction
[1]Viktor E. Frankl, *Man's Search for Meaning* (Boston: Beacon, 1959), p. 113.

Week Four: The Good News Changes Lives
[1]Roger Steer, *Basic Christian: The Inside Story of John Stott* (Downers Grove, IL: InterVarsity Press, 2010), pp. 33-35.

Week Five: The Good News Is for Everyone
[1]Leighton Ford, *The Attentive Life: Discerning God's Presence in All Things* (Downers Grove, IL: InterVarsity Press, 2008).

Week Six: The First Mission Trip
[1]Henry T. Blackaby and Claude V. King, *Experiencing God* (Nashville, TN: Broadman and Holman, 1994), p. 120 .
[2]Often attributed to St. Augustine, the quote originated in a tract on Christian unity by German Lutheran theologian Rupertis Meldenius, *Paraenesis votiva pro pace ecclesiae ad theologos Augustanae Confessionis*, circa 1627.

Week Seven: More Mission Trips
[1]John Stott, *The Message of Acts* (Downers Grove, IL: InterVarsity Press, 1990), p. 283; F. F. Bruce, "The Acts of the Apostles," in *The New Bible Commentary: Revised*, ed. Donald Guthrie and Alec Motyer (Grand Rapids: Eerdmans, 1970), p. 996.

Week Eight: Paul's Journey to Jerusalem
[1]John Stott, *The Message of Acts* (Downers Grove, IL: InterVarsity Press, 1990), p. 342.

[2]David McCasland, *Oswald Chambers: Abandoned to God* (Charlotte, NC: Billy Graham Evangelistic Association, 1997), p. 175.

[3]Fanny J. Crosby, "Blessed Assurance," 1873.

[4]F. F. Bruce, "The Acts of the Apostles," in *The New Bible Commentary: Revised*, ed. Donald Guthrie and Alec Motyer (Grand Rapids: Eerdmans, 1970), p. 1004.

[5]Reinhold Niebuhr, *The Essential Reinhold Niebuhr: Selected Essays and Addresses* (New Haven, CT: Yale University Press, 1986), p. 251.

Week Nine: Paul's Roman Trial

[1]John Stott, *The Message of Acts* (Downers Grove, IL: InterVarsity Press, 1990), pp. 359-60.

Week Ten: Paul's Journey to Rome

[1]For more Bible reading help see pages 141-42 of this book or go to www .scriptureunionresources.com.

[2]John Stott, *The Message of Acts* (Downers Grove, IL: InterVarsity Press, 1990), p. 405.

THE ESSENTIAL QUESTION
RESOURCES FOR CHURCHES AND GROUPS

Imagine if your church or group read through the book of Acts together using *The Essential Question*, and then worked together to make a difference for God in your community. Scripture Union has produced a range of resources, based on the book by Whitney T. Kuniholm, to help you do just that. Order the mix that best fits your needs.

Devotional Book
+ 50 devotional commentaries through Acts
+ 10 sets of group discussion questions
+ The Essential Question Journal
+ And more...

Study Guide
+ 50 mini-studies through Acts
+ 10 sets of group discussion questions

Bible Reading Planner
+ List of 50 readings through Acts
+ Personal Action Plan
+ Track-your-progress Punch-out Card

To learn more and receive special discounts, go to:
SCRIPTUREUNIONRESOURCES.COM

scriptureunion
RESOURCES
YOUR BIBLE ENGAGEMENT PARTNER

OTHER ESSENTIAL BIBLE READING PROGRAMS

Scripture Union has other Essential Bible Reading Resources for individuals, groups and churches. Here's why they work so well: Short readings... perfect for busy people. Undated...no one falls behind, no one feels guilty. Sermon-friendly...download free sermons for every passage. *Plus, all Essential Bible Reading Resources work with any Bible translation.*

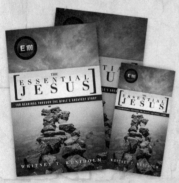

The Essential Jesus

The story of salvation in 25 Old Testament and 75 New Testament readings

+ Devotional Book by Whitney T. Kuniholm
+ Study Guide
+ Bible Reading Planner
+ Youth Editions available

Also available from Scripture Union is *The Essential 100*.

To learn more and receive special discounts, go to:
SCRIPTUREUNIONRESOURCES.COM